ADOPTION WISDOM

Guid _____ _____ *and*

_____ _____ *ion*

Praise for Adoption Wisdom

"Take heed with open eyes, ears, and heart! This book maps the wisdom of lifelong-trained experts: Those who are walking and feeling the convoluted, intergenerational path of adoption."
LaVonne H. Stiffler, Ph.D., author of <u>Synchronicity and Reunion</u>

"ADOPTION WISDOM is a succinct overview of the adoption experience made personal by the many quotes used to teach the issues. It is quite easily readable while it explains complex life challenges."
Sharon Kaplan Roszia, co-author of <u>The Open Adoption Experience</u>

"A treasure among adoption books. For all those involved in the lifelong relationships of adoption."
Stephanie E. Siegel, Ph.D., author of <u>Parenting Your Adopted Child</u>

"The voices whose lives are touched by adoption speak out. A valued contribution to the growing literature on adoption."
Reuben Pannor, co-author of <u>The Adoption Triangle</u> and <u>Lethal Secrets</u>

"Dr. Russell has given us a wide-ranging book clearly reflecting both personal and professional experience."
Annette Baran, co-author of <u>The Adoption Triangle</u> and <u>Lethal Secrets</u>

"ADOPTION WISDOM is a wonderful and poignant addition to post-adoption literature. With Dr. Russell as a thoughtful and gentle guide, each page is a beautiful blend of voices of all who are affected by adoption. From their combined dialogue, one cannot escape the notion that perhaps the true gift of adoption is the wisdom and insight one gains by merely 'participating' in this life-long process."
Jean A. S. Strauss, author of <u>Birthright: The Guide to Search and Reunion</u> and <u>The Great Adoptee Search Book</u>

ADOPTION WISDOM

A Guide to the Issues and Feelings of Adoption

Marlou Russell, Ph.D.

BROKEN BRANCH PRODUCTIONS
Santa Monica, California 2010

Publisher's Cataloging in Publication
(Prepared by Quality Books, Inc.)

Adoption wisdom: a guide to the issues and feelings of adoption
  / Marlou Russell.
    p. cm.
    Includes bibliographical references.
    LCCN: 96-96069
    ISBN: 1-888511-12-5.

    1. Adoption--Psychological aspects. I. Title.
HV875.R87 1996   362.7'34
                                    QBI96-20157

Cover Design: Lightbourne Images
Author Photograph: David Peevers

ISBN 1-888511-12-5   Converted ISBN 978-1-88511-12-3

Library of Congress Catalog Card Number: 96-96069

Printed in the United States of America

First Printing: 1996

10 9 8 7 6 5

BROKEN BRANCH PRODUCTIONS
1452 26th Street, Suite 103
Santa Monica, CA 90404

Dedication

To those who have not yet found their voice

Wisdom: *accumulated philosophic or scientific learning -* **knowledge.** *ability to discern inner qualities and relationships -* **insight.** *good sense - judgment. a wise attitude or course of action. the teachings of the ancient wise men. sny - see* **sense.**

A Note to the Reader

Acknowledgments

My thanks to the many people and organizations who have inspired me and added to my knowledge about adoption: Robert Anderson, Annette Baran, Betty Jean Lifton, Reuben Pannor, Joyce McGuire Pavao, Sharon Kaplan Roszia, Carol Schaefer, Stephanie Siegel, Joe Soll, Jean Strauss, Lavonne Stiffler, Thomas Verny, Nancy Verrier, Linda Yellin, AAC, ALMA, CERA, and CUB.

A hearty thank you to Monica Faulkner for her editorial assistance; to Susan Picking Harper for her graphic design suggestions; and to Janet Andrews for her support and encouragement.

My thanks to the clients, students, and triad members I have known who showed me the need for this book. A special thank you to those who took the time to write about their adoption experiences - I was moved and touched by each letter.

To my husband, Jan, who knows when to nudge and when to just listen - thank you for your strength and comfort.

And to my adoptive family and birth family - there is a place for all of you in my heart and in my life.

Preface

Adoption has always been a part of my life. I was adopted as an infant in a closed adoption. I was not supposed to meet my birth family and they were never to know me. Like many adoptees, I always knew I was adopted and was told that being adopted meant being special and being chosen.

Growing up, I had lots of questions and fantasies about my origins. Who was my birth mother and why had she given me up? What was my medical history? What was my nationality? Would I ever meet anyone who looked like me?

I searched and found my birth mother. She was afraid to look for me because she did not know if I knew I was adopted. She had thought about me often but didn't know if she had the right to contact me. She says the day I called was the happiest day of her life.

My journey of search, reunion and healing led me to adoption support groups, conferences, books, and conversations with triad members. I began to specialize in working with triad members in my psychotherapy practice and teach classes on the lifelong impact of adoption. This book is based on material I present in the classes and on what I have learned about adoption over the years.

My purpose in writing this book is threefold: to validate the feelings of triad members; to prepare those who are considering adoption; and to educate people about the lifelong impact of adoption. My hope is that each reader will gain a fuller appreciation of the complexities of the adoption experience.

CONTENTS

1: The Adoption Triad

"I wish I knew then what I know now."   *Birth parent*

Adoption Beliefs

Adoption forces people to embrace a certain set of beliefs. Adoptive parents need to believe that there is no difference between adoptive and biological parenting. Birth parents need to believe that they will get over relinquishing their child for adoption. Adoptees need to believe that they are better off in their adoptive home than if they had stayed in their birth family. Without these beliefs, adoption would probably not take place.

This book addresses some basic beliefs about adoption. It is meant to be a simple book about a complex topic. Not everyone who reads this book will agree with everything here. The issues raised in these pages may surprise some people. Others will be glad to read what they have been feeling all along.

The quotations in this book are from people who are living the adoption experience. The author distributed a flier asking triad members how they had been affected by adoption and what they wanted people to know about the realities of adoption. Participation was anonymous although many people stated that their identities could be used. The quotations seen here are from those who took the time to share their thoughts and feelings about adoption.

Adoption Triad Members

"It is so strange to know that I am related to people I have never seen. Somewhere out there are people that share my bloodlines and genetic characteristics. I may never meet them but they are still a part of my life."   *Adoptee*

"I think about my son a lot. It was hard to let him go but I know deep in my heart that it was the best for him. I'm glad I will be able to know how he is over the years. I can't imagine never seeing him again."   Birth parent

"Our world changed with Jessica. Now we are a family."
Adoptive parent

The adoption triad consists of the adoptee, the birth parents, and the adoptive parent or parents. Every adoption involves these three participants whether they personally know each other or not. Like any triangle, all parts are necessary and support each other. Adoption triad members are linked to each other for the rest of their lives. They share a bond and relationships that cannot be severed by time, distance, or denial.

Terms for Triad Members

"When I was growing up people would ask me where my real parents were. I told them at home."   Adoptee

Using the term "real" or "natural" to describe a parent is offensive. If one parent is real, than the other parent would be unreal. There are no "unreal" or "unnatural" parents.

The language that we use can be very powerful. Words *can* hurt people emotionally. In an area like adoption, it is very important to use words and terms that are respectful and nonjudgmental.

In adoption, the terms "mother" and "father" describe the adoptive parents. Sometimes the adjective "adoptive" is added for clarification purposes if talking about the adoptive family and the birth family. Typically, in a conversational setting, an adoptee will say "mother" and "father" when referring to his or her parents and "birth mother" and "birth father" to refer to his or her birth parents.

The terms "birth mother" and "birth father" describe the birth parents or the biological parents. Using these terms for the birth parents allows society to have a title and place for birth parents. Just as we have terms and a place for grandparents and stepparents, birth parents fit in with our language. It is similar to grandmother and stepfather - people who we honor by having terms for them.

The term "adoptee" is the preferred term to describe someone who is adopted. It is a word that has no age limits. Sometimes adoptees are referred to as adopted children. This sounds ridiculous when the adoptee is fifty years old! Adoptees are people of many ages.

Beyond the Triad

"What society doesn't get is that I didn't just lose my birth mother and birth father. I also lost my grandparents, aunts and uncles, cousins and siblings."   Adoptee

It is said that for every adoption that takes place, fifteen people are affected. Not only are the primary triad members affected, but so are the people related to them. This includes the birth and adoptive grandparents, aunts, uncles, cousins, brothers, and sisters of the birth and adoptive parents, and any siblings of the adoptee.

"I had to change jobs. The pulling and tugging and decisions of adoption were too much for me to handle after a while. I'm glad I had the experience but I spent as much time as I could there."
                    Former adoption professional

The professionals who are involved in adoptions can also be affected by the emotional environment. Social workers, attorneys, and judges can feel the impact of adoption situations. Separating and recreating families is hard work that has a strong emotional component.

"I watched my mother as tears streamed down her face. This was her first grandchild. She didn't want me to release my child for adoption. I knew that this adoption would forever change my entire family. And it has!"   Birth parent

For many birth grandparents, adoption means that they are losing their first grandchild and will not have the pleasure of watching him or her grow up. Other family members affected are brothers and sisters of both the birth parents and the adoptive parents. Aunts, uncles, cousins, and others may also feel the effects of adoption, especially if adoption has been considered a "family secret."

"I want people to know there are other innocent victims of adoption. If I had been told that my first son (who I gave up for adoption) was OK, then I could have raised my second son with more confidence and less worry. I believe that my second son picked up my fears and anxiety and it has impacted him greatly."   Birth parent

"When I saw a baby, I would think about how old our baby would have been had he lived. Even though I miscarried, I still can feel the effects of our lost child."   Adoptive parent

Phantom children can be very loud and present in people's lives. It is virtually impossible to forget having a child or having difficulty conceiving a child. Acknowledging these facts and experiences allows healing to take place. Respecting these losses honors the people and souls who have had such impact on one's life regardless of the amount of actual contact. To ignore or deny these losses can lead to trying to replace the lost person or halting the necessary grieving process.

Pain

"It's hard to describe exactly what the feelings are. All I know is that it is always there - this pain that feels constant and dull or sharp and unbearable."   *Adoptee*

Pain is a very real part of adoption. Triad members and other people sometimes overlook the pain of adoption. It is expected that adoption is a happy event in which everyone gets their needs met and everything works out for the best. As wonderful as adoption can be, there will also be some painful feelings. Pain can take the form of feeling sad, lonely, angry, frustrated, or even suicidal. Some adoptees experience a longing to fit in and belong. Some birth parents feel a sense of guilt and shame. Some adoptive parents feel frustrated and confused about their adopted children, and wonder what their own biological children would have been like.

"Sometimes I'm in so much pain, I don't know what to do. I just want to forget that it happened. I want to get on with my life and not be so sad and depressed."   *Birth parent*

Once the pain of adoption is acknowledged, it can be understood and the healing process can begin. You cannot heal something you do not admit exists. Acknowledging the pain can be as simple as allowing yourself to feel sad and not judging yourself for your feelings. Some people find the acknowledgment they need in support groups of other adoptees, birth parents, or adoptive parents.

Understanding the Pain

"I was overjoyed when my daughter told me she was pregnant. I'm really looking forward to being a grandmother. But I find myself crying lately and I'm not sure why. I think I'm sad that I never gave birth and that I won't be able to share that experience with my daughter."   Adoptive parent

Understanding pain means validating and accepting whatever feelings arise, whenever they arise. It is crucial to have a safe space to express feelings where there is no judgment. Feelings are neither right nor wrong; they just are. Being a part of adoption means having feelings that may seem difficult to experience and understand.

2: The History of Adoption

"Adoption sure isn't what it used to be!!"   *Adoption attorney*

Changes Over Time

"I know logically that my birth mother couldn't have kept me. It was 1958 and single women just didn't keep their babies then. She tells me that her parents would not have helped her out at all, that she didn't have a job. But it still hurts, the fact that she gave me away. I know it's not fair, but I keep thinking that she could have done <u>something</u> to have kept me."   *Adoptee*

"I go over it and over it in my head. Was there a way to have kept my baby? I know the answer is no but I keep blaming myself. I think, 'How could anyone give away their baby?' I feel so much guilt. But I have to keep reminding myself that there was no choice for me then. I couldn't support myself, let alone a baby too! I wish it had been different. I'm still living with the consequences of that difficult decision."   *Birth parent*

"Adoption is so different these days. When we adopted David thirty years ago, there was no fear about the birth mother or worry about how David would turn out. My gynecologist had told me about a girl who was pregnant and looking for a home for her baby. He knew I wanted kids but couldn't have any, so it all worked out."   *Adoptive parent*

Adoption has gone through many changes in the last few years. Although thousands of children need homes, adoption attracts people who want to adopt newborn infants. In the past there were more babies who needed homes than there were people who wanted to be adoptive parents. Now the reverse is true, there are more people wanting to be adoptive parents than babies who need homes. This shift has many causes. The use of birth control and the availability of abortion have decreased the number of unwanted pregnancies. Also, single women can now decide to keep their babies without the social stigma of the past.

Solution to Problems

"On the surface, it seems like such a win-win situation for everyone."   *Adoption professional*

"I didn't know what to do. My boyfriend had left me, my parents disowned me, and I didn't have a job. How could I raise a child?"   *Birth parent*

"I needed to be raised by someone."   *Adoptee*

"We wanted a child more than anything else in the world."
                    Adoptive parent

Initially, adoption was considered to be a simple solution to everyone's problems. The problems were: 1) a birth parent was pregnant and unable to parent a child at this time, 2) a baby would need a home and parents, and 3) infertile parents wanted a child to raise. It seemed that adoption was a workable solution for all parties involved.

"Now I know that we should have talked about the adoption more than we did. No one told us that it would be an issue."
                    Adoptive parent

"They kept telling me that I couldn't raise my baby. They said that a child needs two parents. They told me I would get on with my life and forget. I believed them."   *Birth parent*

"My parents told me that I was chosen, that my birth mother decided on adoption because it was the best for me."   *Adoptee*

The main focus of adoptions in the past was the matching of babies and adoptive parents. There was typically no training, education, or information given to adoptive parents. Any counseling that birth parents received was usually from social workers at the adoption agency whose job was to find babies for their clients, the adoptive parents.

The adoptee was transferred to the adoptive parents, the adoption was legalized, and the birth family and the adoptive family went their separate ways. Adoptive parents were told to raise their adopted child as if it were their own biological child. Birth parents were told to put the experience behind them. Adoptees were told that being adopted meant being "chosen" and "special." The adoption may or may not ever have been discussed again in the adoptive family or the birth family.

Problems Arose

"I just wanted to see someone who looked like me."   Adoptee

"People told me that I would 'forget' about my baby and that my life could then go ahead as if I had never been pregnant. I don't know about other people, but I could never forget about my baby and my life could never go back to what it was before I was pregnant."   Birth parent

"No one told us that adoptees sometimes have difficulty with times of separation. I never thought we'd get through that first day of kindergarten!"   Adoptive parent

Problems arose for many triad members. Issues surfaced that no one had talked about before. Birth parents found they were having trouble "forgetting" that they had had a child. Adoptees wanted more information about their biological families. Adoptive parents were experiencing difficulties in raising their children that no one had warned them about.

Triad members became more vocal about their feelings and needs. Support groups began and provided a place where adoptees, birth parents, and adoptive parents could reveal and validate their feelings.

Formation of Support Groups

"It took me a long time to get to my first ALMA meeting. I was told about the group by a friend and joined without even going to a meeting. It was so overwhelming to get the first newsletter in the mail. I cried and cried, seeing all the reunion pictures. It was wonderful and painful."   Adoptee

"I remember seeing the notice in the newspaper for the CUB meeting. I couldn't believe that people would get together and talk about what we were all told not to talk about! It took me a few months to get up the courage to actually attend my first meeting but when I did I was so relieved to be with people who understood. I hadn't talked with anyone about giving up my baby since the adoption twenty-five years ago."   Birth parent

As triad members became more vocal about their feelings and needs, support groups began to take shape. Support groups gave people a place to talk with others about their concerns, feelings and issues of shared interest. Support groups have changed adoption by giving triad members a stronger collective voice. There are support groups for each triad position and groups that are open to all triad members.

Sealed Records

"It's hard to start out with deception. My own birth certificate lies about who I am. Talk about identity issues!"   Adoptee

In adoption, the original birth certificate of the adoptee is sealed by law after an amended birth certificate is produced. The adoptee's original birth certificate contains the name and information of the birth mother and may list information about the birth father. The adoptee may be given a first name by the birth parent on the original birth certificate and will have the last name of a birth parent. If not given a first name, the adoptee will be known as Baby (birth parent's last name).

"My life began with a lie. They still won't tell me the truth."

Adoptee

The amended birth certificate replaces the original birth certificate and lists the adoptive parents' information as if they were the biological parents. The original birth certificate is sealed by the courts and can not be released except by court order.

"It seems like a crime that everyone else can walk into a courthouse and ask a clerk for their original birth certificate and get it, but I can't. Where are my rights?"   *Adoptee*

Adoptees are the only Americans who do not have access to their original birth certificates. If an adoptee requests his or her original birth certificate, they will be told it is off-limits to them and will receive a copy of their amended birth certificate.

"How can the courts say they are a justice system searching for the truth when they won't even give me my own birth certificate?"   *Adoptee*

Originally, records were sealed to protect all the parties involved. It was thought that an adoptee born out of wedlock would suffer societal consequences. It was felt that birth mothers needed privacy about the fact that they had been pregnant. Amended birth certificates allowed adoptive parents to act as if they had given birth to their child and protected them from the stigma of infertility and adoption.

Open versus Closed Adoption

"As an adoptee from a closed adoption, I am envious of the wealth of information that is currently available to the children of open adoption. In open adoption, birth parents are encouraged to write letters to their children and adoptive parents agree to send pictures of the child to the agency to be passed on to the birth parents. How I wish that I had been able to exchange information with my birth family and they with me thirty four years ago. Perhaps my life would be quite different. Perhaps not .I will never know."   Adoptee

The traditional closed adoptions of the past meant that birth families and adoptive families were not to communicate with each other. Intermediaries such as social workers, attorneys, or doctors were the communication links between the two families. It was expected that no direct contact would take place before or after the adoption proceedings.

"Closed adoption is a very traumatizing experience. Open adoption seems to me to be a better alternative. The belief that a child can simply be cut off from his or her birth parents and grafted onto another family with no contact between the biological parent and child from then on is a belief that is not grounded in reality. Not only are there medical reasons for allowing access to adoption records, there are emotional and spiritual reasons for that connection to be maintained."

Birth parent

Open adoption is a relatively new option in adoption practice. At first thought to be a progressive and unique way of adopting, it is now becoming the chosen style of adoption if not yet the norm in adoption practices.

"I wanted to know where my baby was going to end up. I wanted to make sure he would have a better life than I could give him. It was hard to choose adoptive parents but I feel good knowing who they are and that we will stay in touch."

Birth parent

"I didn't want an open adoption in the beginning. I wanted to be the only mother. There have been some rough spots but many joys too. Sometimes I feel that we have adopted a child and a mother. Communication is key. If we can all love this beautiful baby boy, then we will have done a good job of parenting."

Adoptive parent

Current open adoption practices involve birth parents choosing who will be the adoptive parents for their child, communicating over the years, and deciding on the kind and amount of contact that shall be maintained.

"We thought we were going to have an open adoption where the birth mother would send a birthday card to our son and we would send pictures once a year. In the beginning, she called us a lot, crying, to find out how Jason was. It was really difficult for us, so we had to be firm about our original agreement with her about contact. Now, four years later, things have calmed down. We send her pictures of Jason, and she writes him a letter on his birthday."

Adoptive parent

There are different definitions and agreements about how open an open adoption will actually be. Sometimes an open adoption means only that the birth parents choose the adoptive parents. Other times, it means that communication will be maintained between the birth family and adoptive family over the course of the adoptee's life.

"It felt really strange to sign a contract about how often we would have contact with the birth parents. Since the birth father also wanted contact, we had to negotiate with him and the birth

mother separately. It took some doing to get everyone to agree. It also took some time to get comfortable with the idea that these people would be in our lives forever."   Adoptive parent

Sometimes the initial expectations of an open adoption arrangement are changed either by agreement or by default. It is a good idea to get social security numbers from the other triad members so you can always find them. In addition, a written agreement signed by the birth parents and the adoptive parents will clarify communication expectations.

"Our daughter's birth mother is very willing to communicate and keeps in touch. Our son's birth mother has just drifted away and we don't know where she is now. It's hard to explain to our son why his birth mother hasn't written him."
                                                    Adoptive parent

Perhaps the most challenging aspect of open adoption is ongoing communication. Emotions are a very real aspect of adoption and will impact communication. The pain of adoption can be so great that a triad member may need to take a break from the relationship, with or without an explanation of his or her absence. Sometimes assumptions, fears, and sadness need to be discussed again to clarify expectations and feelings.

"The adoptee is the one that has the easiest time accepting an open adoption. I think it's the adoptive parents and the birth parents who struggle with it the most."   *Adoption professional*

Perhaps the most important principle to keep in mind whether the adoption is open or closed is that adoption is for the child. The adults involved need to sometimes put their personal feelings aside to consider what is in the best interest of the adoptee.

3: Basic Truths of Adoption

"It was such a relief to hear someone say what I had been feeling in my heart for so long."   *Adoptee*

Lifelong Impact
"I keep thinking that I have dealt with all my adoption issues but then another one comes along - bang - and I realize that there is more work to be done."   *Adoptee*

Adoption is more than a single event in time marked by the signing of the adoption decree; it has lifelong consequences for all triad members.

"I wanted to believe the social workers and my mother that I would forget giving my baby up for adoption. It's never gone away, though, and at this point, I'm not sure that it ever will."
Birth parent

Even though the legal aspects of adoption are time-limited, the emotional aspects of adoption continue throughout each triad member's life. Sometimes a simple question or a newspaper article will trigger adoption-related emotions and thoughts.

"You would think that by this time things would not still affect me. I was shopping for a baby shower gift and found myself being quite sad that I had never given birth."   *Adoptive parent*

It is difficult, if not impossible, to shield one's self from the lifelong impact of adoption. Becoming aware of the emotional issues of adoption and embracing them enables people to work through their feelings, express them, and resolve them to the best of their ability.

Creating Families/Separating Families

"I didn't really think about all the ramifications of this adoption on the birth family. I felt as if we were finally getting the child we wanted and that we were helping out someone who was in a difficult situation."   *Adoptive parent*

To create an adoptive family, a birth family must be separated. This is one of the emotional and logistical laws of adoption. There is no getting around this fact. Even in adoptions in which a relative's family adopts the adoptee, the original birth family is disrupted and the adoptee is displaced.

"I don't want my status as an adoptee to highlight all that my adoptive parents did for me while denying my birth family. Both families are a part of me and always will be."   *Adoptee*

The way to integrate and honor both families in adoption is to acknowledge that they both exist and accept that they are both crucial to the structure of adoption. Each family brings to adoption what the other family could not.

Second Choice for All

"If I had my choice, I would choose not to be an adoptee. I would choose to be born into a biological family that celebrated my birth. I would choose to have a mother who wanted me and could love me unconditionally."   *Adoptee*

"I never wanted to surrender my baby. I really thought that my parents would be there for me and that they would help me raise my daughter. I was stunned and hurt when they sent me to the home for unwed mothers. But even in the home, I believed that I would keep my child. I still can't get over the fact that I signed those papers and that somebody I don't know is raising my child."   *Birth parent*

"We tried to get pregnant for four years. It never occurred to us that it would be so hard. We went through all the infertility treatments and got totally burned out both emotionally and financially. It took us a while to get used to the idea of adoption. But when we sat down and really talked about whether we wanted to raise a child, we agreed that we still wanted to. That was when we started finding out about adoption."

Adoptive parent

Adoption is a second choice for all the triad members. People do not expect to grow up, get married, and adopt a child. They expect to grow up, get married, and have their own biological children. Likewise, a person does not expect to grow up, get pregnant, and give their child to strangers to raise. It is also expected that families will retain their kinship ties and grow up knowing their biological relatives.

"I know I was better off having been adopted. I don't always like being an adoptee, but I've learned a lot and I'm a stronger person because of it."   *Adoptee*

Adoption as a second choice does not necessarily mean that adoption is less than or not as good as non-adoption choices. Taking an alternative path can sometimes lead to amazing experiences and growth that would not have been possible if the original road were taken.

Babies Are Aware

"I was all ready to get an abortion, but then I read a book on how a baby develops and what is happening when you are pregnant. I kind of flipped out when I realized that this was a person already. I couldn't go through with the abortion."

Birth parent

It was once thought that babies were not aware of their surroundings or the people around them before and after birth. What has become more and more clear through research is that babies are aware. Pre- and perinatal psychology includes pregnancy as a time of awareness for the developing fetus.

"I was at a rock concert when I was eight months pregnant. I had to leave because my baby was kicking me so much. I guess he didn't like the band very much!"   Birth parent

If you go to any bookstore, you will find books on how to bond better with your baby before birth. More and more, people are realizing that a maturing fetus has the capacity to take in more than just nutrition. Newborn infants can recognize voices heard while in utero. Children can be calmed by hearing the same music they heard while their mother was pregnant with them. Babies can express their displeasure at what their mother is doing by kicking in the womb.

"It's hard to describe but when Susan (the birth mother) comes over to visit Shane he just connects to her in a way that he doesn't with me. I don't know if it is her voice or her mannerisms or what, but there is definitely something between them."   Adoptive parent

Bonding is a biological and emotional process that happens between a pregnant woman and her developing baby during pregnancy. The degree of bonding and the quality of bonding are important to the health of the baby. It is not a question of *whether* a pregnant woman will bond with her baby; it is a question of *how* she will bond with her baby. Pregnant women constantly express and transmit feelings to their developing babies. A pregnant woman who will raise her child and a pregnant woman who will not raise her child will both be conveying messages to their unborn children.

"I remember I just kept rubbing my stomach and telling my baby that I was sorry that I couldn't keep her. I cried a lot and slept a lot during my pregnancy. My baby was pretty quiet, not kicking or anything. I kept telling her that I wished we could be together and that maybe we would someday."   Birth parent

Women who have chosen adoption for their babies can usually tell you about their bonding experiences with their babies while they were pregnant. Even though a pregnant woman knows she will be releasing her baby for adoption, she can still feel a connection to her child as only a mother can.

"I've done some therapy where I've gone back to some prenatal experiences. It was very difficult but also very revealing in that I could feel the feelings of that time when my birth mother was pregnant with me. I felt very sad and helpless. I feel like it was her sadness and my sadness all at the same time. Later, when I met my birth mother, I asked her about that time. She started crying a lot and saying that she was really sad then. She said she tried not to 'talk' to me while she was pregnant because she knew she couldn't keep me and she didn't want to feel too connected."   Adoptee

Throughout their lives, adoptees feel some kind of connection to the mother who gave them birth. These feelings of connection, no matter how repressed or forgotten, are present throughout the life of both the mother and her child. This is the bond in adoption that inspires adoptees and birth parents to search for each other.

Nature versus Nurture

"When my friends talk about being so much like their mother or aunt or someone else in their biological family, it makes me wonder if I would be like my birth mother. I feel as if I do share some characteristics with my adoptive mother, but I know I'll never look like her or be like her in lots of ways."   Adoptee

The long-standing question of nature versus nurture continues to be addressed in scientific circles and in society at large. This debate has special significance in adoption. People want to know how much of a child's personality and behavior is due to genetics and how much is due to the way the child is being raised.

"I am very artistic and my adoptive family was not. They just couldn't understand my need to create and do my art. They thought I was flaky and always wanted me to take classes in school that would help me get a 'regular' job later in life. They didn't get that art was going to be my career. When I met my birth family, it was a real joy to be around people who understood and were artistic themselves."   *Adoptee*

"There have been these really terrible movies about adopted kids being terrors in their adoptive families - setting fires to their homes and being totally unmanageable. It's like the bad seed theory meets Freddy Krueger. Sometimes people ask me if I am ever afraid of my adopted son. I say 'No, are you ever afraid of your son?' That usually shuts them up."   *Adoptive parent*

Perhaps the most useful way to look at the nature versus nurture question is to understand that both parts are important and contribute to the personality of each individual. We will probably never know exactly how much effect genetics has compared to the environment. To test the nature versus nurture theory, twin babies would have to be separated from their mother at birth and raised in separate families. Not many people would support that kind of research. However, the twin research that has been done has shown remarkable similarities among twin pairs.

Loss for All Triad Members
"How can I ever get over the fact that I gave up my first child for adoption? It's hard not knowing where she is and if she is OK or not."   *Birth parent*

"I may never know anyone who is biologically related to me. It's mind-boggling and extremely sad."   Adoptee

"Our therapist had us do a ceremony about burying our fantasy biological child. It was really emotional. I resisted doing it for a long time and then I realized that we needed to let go and move on with the adoption. Holding on to the hope of having a biological child was holding us back."   Adoptive parent

Adoption inherently involves loss for all the triad members. The birth parent loses a child, the adoptee loses biological ties, and the adoptive parent loses the hope of having a biological child. Acknowledgment of the losses of adoption and the grieving for these losses is crucial for all triad members.

4: Loss and Grief in Adoption

"It's a loss that lives on and on."   *Birth parent*

Loss and Grief

"There's a hole inside of me, an empty space that can only be filled by my birth mother, wherever she may be."   *Adoptee*

"I thought I'd be OK after a while. I expected some sadness. I just didn't think I'd miss her so much."   *Birth parent*

"My daughter still blames me for her having to give her child up for adoption. What she doesn't realize is that I too feel sad. I lost my first grandchild. We just couldn't see any other way to handle the situation. I still cry about it sometimes."

       Birth grandparent

Grief is a natural reaction to experiencing a loss. Grieving is a healing process that takes courage and vulnerability. Loss and grief are core issues in adoption.

"We were so happy when we brought Nikki home. She was adorable and sweet and such a treasure! Later, as I sat holding her, I thought about Debbie, her birth mother, and how much Debbie was going to miss her. I started crying and feeling sad for Debbie's loss. Here we were so happy to have little Nikki, and there was Debbie, home alone without the baby she had carried for nine months."   *Adoptive parent*

The need for grieving can be overlooked by triad members and those around them because adoption is typically seen as a positive event and solution. The decision to adopt or to release a child is an emotionally draining experience. By the time the birth and adoption actually take place, people can be exhausted. The focus becomes on the present and the future. The adoptive parents become busy raising their child, the birth parents attempt to move on in their lives, and the adoptee gets used to new caretakers.

"I think back to what it must have been like for me as a baby to be alone, scared, not knowing where I was or where my mother was. What a tremendous loss."   Adoptee

"No one seemed to realize that the depression I was feeling for all these years might have been connected to surrendering my child for adoption. I went to three different therapists, but we never really talked about how my being a birth mother could have contributed to my depression. It was only after being in a support group of birth mothers that I realized we were all depressed to some extent."   Birth parent

If grieving is not given its rightful place in the process of adoption, physical and emotional symptoms may occur at the time of adoption or later in life. Some people describe their emotional symptoms as sadness, anxiety, loss of interest in activities, sleeping more than usual, and depression. Other people become alerted to their emotional issues when physical symptoms appear. Regardless of how signs and symptoms appear, unless loss is recognized, grieving can not take place.

Kubler-Ross Stages of Grief

"Death doesn't scare me. I have always been drawn to death in some kind of way. I know that sounds strange! I always wanted to figure it out and I have always been able to be there for people who are grieving the loss of someone who has died. Sometimes I wonder if I'm interested in grief because I lost my birth mother when I was born."   Adoptee

Elisabeth Kubler-Ross has been a pioneer in the field of death and dying research. In her work with dying people and those close to them, she has identified five stages of the normal grieving process. These five stages can be worked through in any order. Some stages may be revisited, but typically people pass through all five stages in their processing of grief issues.

Denial

"It's amazing how many people in my support group experienced the same things that I did as an adoptee. One night we talked about how none of us believed that adoption had affected us. Even after my birth mother found me, I told her that I had not ever felt sad about being adopted. Now, looking back, I can't believe it. Talk about denial!!! How about being in denial all my life?"
                                                              Adoptee

"I think I started my grieving process for my daughter when I first became pregnant with her. I denied that I was pregnant for five months. When I started to show, my mother asked me if I was pregnant. I said 'No.' After I gave birth I was kind of numb and still couldn't fully fathom what was happening. Even to this day, that time in my life is a little blurry. Maybe I need it to be that way."
                                                          Birth parent

"It never crosses our mind that Eric is adopted."

                                                       Adoptive parent

The first stage of grieving is denial. Feeling shock, disbelief, numb, and detached is common. The incident or feelings are kept out of one's awareness. Denial is protective in that it helps people to function when the truth or clarity would be too much to handle. Staying in denial, however, has negative consequences. To ignore important issues and feelings is like having an elephant in the living room that no one talks about. Everyone walks around it and pretends it isn't there even though it's in the way of everything.

Anger

"I'm still really angry at the social worker and the agency. The agency never talked with me about any options. They told me that if I really loved my child, I would give it up for adoption. No one said anything about welfare or how to get a job and raise my child."   Birth parent

"At one point, I felt myself getting angry at anyone who was pregnant. It felt so unfair that other people could get pregnant (and some of them without even trying!) while my husband and I had tried for so many years."   Adoptive parent

The second stage of grieving is anger. Anger is the feeling that a situation is unfair and should not have happened. It is common in the anger stage to look for someone to blame other than oneself. Anger can also be very motivating and inspire one to take action. The anger stage can help people start taking better care of themselves or decide to make changes in their life. Many worthwhile organizations have grown out of the energy that anger can produce.

Bargaining

"At the home for unwed mothers, I would think about all the ways that I could keep my baby. I thought that my boyfriend would come and rescue me and our child. I dreamed that my parents would come to visit me and say that they had made a terrible mistake and that I could live at home with them and bring the baby. I asked God to help me. I promised God that if he would help me keep my baby then I would never have sex again."   Birth parent

The third stage of grieving is bargaining. Bargaining involves trying to find ways to undo the situation by searching for trade-offs. Being in the stage of bargaining means that the person is no longer in denial. There is a real awareness of the loss, and the bargaining is an attempt to control a situation that feels out of control.

Depression

"We had gone to so many doctors and gone through so many procedures to get pregnant. We were totally wiped out. Then, when we decided on adoption, it all started again. Probably the time that I was most depressed was when we had talked to three different birth mothers and it didn't seem that anything was going to work out. Once again we were at someone else's mercy."   *Adoptive parent*

"I never thought that it would really get to the point where there were no choices left. I was so depressed. I felt really hopeless about having any kind of say about what would happen to my baby."   *Birth parent*

The fourth stage of grieving is depression. There is a feeling of helplessness and hopelessness about the situation. These feelings may come and go or seem to be constantly present. Depression is the stage that most people associate with the grieving process.

Sometimes physical symptoms such as lack of energy, a change in eating patterns and wanting to sleep a lot can accompany the emotional signs of depression. Some people experience mood changes, inability to concentrate, a feeling of tiredness, a lack of interest in usual activities, and feelings of intense sadness.

It is important to honor this phase of grieving even though it can be a difficult one to experience. Going through the depression will help this stage pass. Trying to avoid the depression means that it will most likely return at a later date.

Acceptance

"I spent so many years wanting it to have been different. I kept wondering what it would have been like to have been raised by

my birth mother. I went through so many phases - being angry, sad, depressed. Finally, I can be in the place where I can see the benefits I got from being adopted. The other feelings are still there from time to time but just not as much as they used to be." Adoptee

"I can't act like it never happened - that I was never pregnant and lost my daughter. I don't want to forget her. But I can try to pick up the pieces and hope and pray that I will someday find her. Maybe when I finally do find her I will feel more at peace."
Birth parent

The fifth and final stage of grieving is acceptance. Acceptance means feeling that the situation is resolved to some extent. The loss is no longer the main focus. There is room for other activities and interests and a balance has been achieved. The goal of acceptance in adoption is not to forget the person or that an adoption has taken place. That would bring one back to the stage of denial. The goal of acceptance is to honor and integrate the people and experience of adoption.

Grieving in Adoption

"Adoption is like having all of your birth family die and getting a replacement family and being told by society how lucky you are that all of your family is dead but we gave you a new one."
Adoptee

Grieving in adoption is different in some distinct ways from mourning the death of someone who has died. When someone dies, there is a definite ending that allows grieving to begin. In adoption, there is no death, no ending. In adoption, a state of limbo exists that is similar to the dynamics of mourning someone who is missing in action. Not knowing where the person is or if they are alive blocks the grieving process. It is difficult to mourn someone who is alive but unavailable.

"I just couldn't forget that I had given birth and agreed to adoption. I would wonder all the time about how she was and where she was. I wondered if anyone would tell me if something bad happened to her. Sometimes I felt really crazy not knowing if she was even alive." Birth parent

"I guess I never really thought about the topic of grieving in adoption. I think I felt that my birth mother and birth family were out there somewhere and that someday we would find each other. I think that if I tried to imagine never meeting them that it would be too devastating. I wanted to believe that we had a connection that could not be broken." Adoptee

Perhaps a similar situation to grieving in adoption is mourning the loss of a relationship in a divorce or separation. An important and primary relationship changes but is not forgotten. Questions about what could have been and fantasies about the possibility of a future are sometimes entertained when relationships are severed. It is not unusual for divorced or separated people to give their relationship another try. Being with someone familiar and comfortable can be reassuring.

"People kept telling us about friends of theirs who had gotten pregnant after they adopted. We finally had to ask people to stop saying it. We knew it wasn't necessarily true, but there was a part of us that wanted to believe it." Adoptive parent

In the case of the fantasy biological child, the adoptive parents can still hold on to the hope that they may one day get pregnant and have a child. Sometimes well-meaning friends urge adoptive parents to hold on to this hope. Keeping the fantasy of a biological child alive will interfere with the mourning process.

"I thought I would be so happy to meet my birth mother - and I was. But I was also very sad - like a depression. I had never really felt depressed about being adopted so it was kind of strange for me to react like I did. I guess that meeting her and meeting my brother and sister made me realize that I had this other family out there. It was like this E-ticket ride up and down - a very amazing experience!"   Adoptee

In adoption, loss and grieving issues can occur and recur at any time. Sometimes people are able to grieve at the time of adoption. For others, the time of search reactivates feelings of helplessness and loss. Some triad members describe reunion as bittersweet, because it brings up previous sad feelings along with the joy of reunion.

"I thought I had pretty much dealt with all the feelings I was going to have about adoption because my son had grown up and was an adult. I didn't expect to be tossed back into that pre-adoption place when my son met his birth mother. I understand their need for reunion, but it sometimes makes me feel left out and I don't always know what to do about that."

Adoptive parent

Regardless of when a triad member feels the feelings of grief, it is important to honor them. Feelings don't always know the difference between past and present. Acknowledging and expressing feelings allows the grieving process to proceed and healing to take place.

5: The Realities of Adoption

"If a mother can love two children, why can't I love two mothers?"
                                                                    Adoptee

The Structure of Adoption

"I've always considered my adoptive parents as my only parents. Now I am trying to incorporate all these new people from my birth family. It can be overwhelming at times."
                                                                    Adoptee

"We thought we would never hear from the woman who gave birth to our daughter. It was quite a surprise when she wrote us a letter and said she wanted to meet our daughter. It took us a long while to feel comfortable with the whole situation."
                                                                    Adoptive parent

The structure of adoption creates relationships that are unique. In adoption, three parties are involved with each other for eternity. Even if the birth family and adoptive family never meet in person, the relationships are created and cemented by the very act of adoption itself.

"My adoptive parents have been great, and I'm really glad they raised me. I had a lot of opportunities growing up. But they can't tell me certain things that only my birth parents could, like where I get my green eyes."
                                                                    Adoptee

Adoptees will always have two sets of parents, the parents who were involved in their creation, and the parents who raised them. Both sets of parents are necessary and play important roles in the life of the adoptee.

"My friends keep trying to understand what it's like to be adopted. They think it's like being in a stepfamily. No one gets upset if you know your mother and your stepmother. But some

people have a problem with me wanting to know my birth mother."   *Adoptee*

Although an adoptive family can be compared to a stepfamily, there are some important differences between the two. In a stepfamily, the continuation of a relationship with the original parent is expected, as is the beginning of a relationship with the stepparent. In an adoptive family, the circumstances of the adoption and the degree of openness determine the amount of contact that the birth family and adoptive family will have. In some adoptive families, it is expected that members of the birth family and the adoptive family will never meet or have any contact. In a stepfamily, by contrast, parents, stepparents, and children are all expected to have some amount of contact with each other.

"I really didn't want to go to the meetings at first. I just wanted to raise Jason and not deal with all the things my wife was bringing up. Going through the adoption was rough enough. I finally did agreed to give the group a try and was surprised that I actually liked it. The kids get to play with each other and we don't have to explain ourselves or answer stupid questions like why Jason doesn't look like us."   *Adoptive parent*

An adoptive family should not try to be what it is not - a biological family. This is not to say that an adoptive family is less than a biological family. It is just different. The differences need to be acknowledged and addressed for the adoptive family to function more smoothly. Unless its unique aspects are understood, adoption will continue to be a round peg being forced into a square hole.

"My family really didn't ever talk about adoption until I told them I wanted to search for my birth mother. Everyone was pretty upset by it, but it turned out to be a way that we could all

talk about what adoption meant to us and to hear what each person felt."   *Adoptee*

There will be many opportunities for the issues and feelings of adoption to be acknowledged and addressed in the adoptive family and the birth family. Choosing adoption means accepting the entire package of adoption, which includes uncomfortable feelings. Bringing up adoption issues can be intimidating, but waiting for them to arise spontaneously can be even more difficult. No matter when or how a family decides to address adoption issues, talking honestly and openly about adoption feelings can create a more communicative environment for everyone in the triad.

Adoption as a Positive Event
"The birth parents benefited from lack of responsibility of a child they did not want or could not care for. The adoptive parents benefited by having a child because they could not have any or wanted more children. Adoptees benefited by usually having a better home than if the birth parents had kept them."
                                                        Adoptee

Adoption is typically seen as a positive event. It is thought that all the triad members will be better off after the adoption takes place. There is much attention given to the next step of bringing the child into the family or moving on from the pregnancy and relinquishment. In reality, all triad members receive something from an adoption, but they also lose something. Feelings about these gains and losses in adoption will present themselves at various times throughout a triad member's life.

Lack of Rituals
"I just went home after I had my baby. It was so strange. Everyone else was acting as if nothing had happened, and for them, nothing had. But for me, my life had changed drastically.

*I went back as a different person to a world that hadn't changed
for anyone but me."*   Birth parent

In the past, there were few if any rituals or ceremonies for
adoption besides the legal proceedings. The birth parents
and the adoptive parents went their separate ways without
acknowledging each other. Ceremonies mark changes and
transitions by honoring what has happened to a person and
between people. Formal ceremonies for events such as
marriage, death, and graduation include people gathering to
offer support and express feelings. We celebrate birthdays
and religious holidays with gifts and appreciation.
Adoption has typically been a quiet and private event that is
meant to go unnoticed.

*"We had heard about people holding ceremonies and thought it
would be a nice way to welcome our baby into our family and
also to acknowledge the emotions and feelings of the birth
parents. We wanted there to be love and appreciation all
around. We all came together and read what we had written
about how we were feeling. There were many tears and also
much happiness. It was really a beautiful ceremony. We have a
videotape of it that we'll be able to show our son to let him know
how loved he was from the very beginning."*   Adoptive parent

Some adoptive parents and birth parents are now creating
their own rituals to honor what is taking place between
them and their child. These ceremonies honor the
importance of the event of adoption and underline the
feelings of each participant in this very emotional
experience.

The Dynamics of Three
*"I really am glad that my daughter has found her birth mother
because I know it meant a lot to her. But sometimes I feel left out*

when I hear that they had a wonderful visit. I worry that my daughter will bond so much with her birth mother that she won't need me anymore."   *Adoptive parent*

"Sometimes I don't tell my adoptive mother about seeing my birth mother because she acts hurt. She doesn't really say anything but she gets this quiet tone in her voice."   *Adoptee*

Whenever there are three people involved in an interaction or relationship specific dynamics will occur. At any one time, it is likely that only two of the three will be in direct contact. The other person will feel left out. This dynamic of two and one can constantly change so that all three people experience being involved and being left out at different times.

"I know it sounds absurd but sometimes I can't stand it when my daughter talks about her adoptive parents and about how things were when she was growing up. I feel so left out - that I missed so much of her life. She was being mothered by someone else and I had wanted to do the mothering - I still do!" Birth parent

Being the one left out in the triad relationship can feel unsettling. It is important to remember that the dynamics of three will constantly change. Each person will get his or her turn at being in direct contact. Each person will also, at times, feel left out. Trusting that these dynamics will change and flow naturally can help keep communication between triad members open.

Confusion
"One of the confusing things for me is I am glad I was adopted, even though my childhood was not a very happy one. Yet I am very sad I did not grow up around my blood relatives. There is a big void in my life due to this."   *Adoptee*

"I'm sorry that I couldn't raise my daughter, but I'm happy that she had a better life than the one I could have given her."
                                                              Birth parent

"We really love Kelly and want the best for her. It's so hard to watch her go through such turmoil. We know we're not to blame for it, but we get confused about what to do sometimes."
                                                          Adoptive parent

Adoption forces triad members to have a mixture of thoughts and feelings that do not seem to fit together. This can lead to a feeling of confusion and an attempt to sort out conflicting messages. Triad members need to allow themselves to experience their full range of thoughts and feelings and not try to force themselves to come to one definitive position.

Mixed Feelings

"I was adopted at the age of three days old by a wonderful man and woman. I had a good life, and my parents taught me all that anybody would be lucky enough to know. I feel I am a very well rounded person with no real hang-ups except that it is very difficult to have that total peace of mind when you cannot know your own family."   *Adoptee*

"It is very difficult to love this precious, beautiful daughter and to feel that the entire evening of her conception was all wrong. But she was meant to be. She was God's will and a part of his big plan. I adored this beautiful baby beyond belief!"
                                                              Birth parent

"She's wonderful and a terror! But I guess any kid would be. It's hard to know how much is adoption and how much isn't. I don't know if any parent is really ready for all that parenthood entails."   *Adoptive parent*

People are capable of feeling many feelings and thinking many thoughts. To think and feel deeply is human. To have mixed feelings is also human and a large part of being an adoption triad member. One of the challenges in adoption is to hold a variety of feelings at the same time.

Wondering

"Sometimes I wonder if there is a predisposition to Alzheimer's or MS or some other crippling disease in my birth family."

Adoptee

"I still wonder how my child is, even though I gave birth to her twenty-three years ago. It never goes away, the wondering."

Birth parent

"I had hoped that we had all the information we needed when we adopted Susan. But now, with the medical condition she has, I wish we could know more to help her and her doctors."

Adoptive parent

In a closed adoption, the triad members do not have the benefit of up-to-date information about the other people in the triad. This can leave a lot of room for wondering, fantasizing, and worrying. It is not uncommon to wonder how another triad member is doing and to want to obtain information that only that person has. Typically, adoptees in closed adoptions do not have access to any of their medical history beyond the health of the birth mother and birth father at the time of the adoption.

Constant Reminders of Adoption

"I dread going to the doctor. Don't they know how awful those medical history forms are for us adoptees?"   *Adoptee*

"Over the years, people have asked me if I have any children. My answer depends on who is asking."   *Birth parent*

"I never know what to say when someone asks about my child's physical characteristics."   Adoptive parent

There can be constant reminders of being a triad member. An adoptee visits a physician for the first time and is asked questions about family medical history. A birth parent is asked how many children she has. A stranger in the grocery store asks an adoptive parent, "Where did your daughter get those beautiful eyes?" In closed adoptions, the answers to these questions are unknown. Each time an innocent question is asked, it once again reminds the triad member of their status as an adoptee, a birth parent, or an adoptive parent.

"I remember being teased about being adopted and not knowing why because my parents had always told me that being adopted meant I was special. Kids would ask me where my 'real' parents were."   Adoptee

The adoptive family can feel much "safer" than the outside world. Sometimes adoptees do not know what to say in response to people's comments and questions. Some adoptees feel the brunt of adoption most strongly in school where kids ask direct questions and tease. School is also where children are asked to do class projects, like drawing a family tree, that confront adoption issues.

"I recall having to do a family history project for a badge in Girl Scouts, and I remember being torn between using my adoptive parents' roots and my own, unknown roots. I asked my parents what I should do, and they said I should forget about wherever I came from because I belonged to them, therefore, their roots were mine. I never completed the project, and that was the only badge I did not receive in Girl Scouts."   Adoptee

Sometimes we think that a childhood experience will be forgotten. But some experiences are forever remembered as a source of discomfort and pain. Living with adoption means being confronted, sometimes on a daily basis, with situations that can have lasting effects.

Secret of Adoption

"Many of my relatives who were not in contact with my adoptive mother when she would have been pregnant with me do not know that I am adopted. Family reunions are interesting because someone will tell me that I look just like my adoptive mother's sister."   *Adoptee*

In some families, adoption is a secret. Some relatives may know about the adoption, while other relatives do not. It becomes difficult to remember who is a part of the secret and who is not.

"I don't know if my parents would have ever told me on their own that I was adopted. I think they got scared that some relative would blurt out the truth, and they felt it was better if I heard it from them. I just wish they had told me before I was fifteen. That was a difficult time to learn about it."   *Adoptee*

Some adoptive parents do not want to tell their child about the adoption but worry that relatives will reveal the secret. Typically, if adoptive parents are not telling their child about being adopted, then there is some issue that the adoptive parent needs to work out.

"I was in shock for quite some time when I found out I was adopted. I then felt this kind of peaceful feeling of understanding events that had happened in my life. It all started to make sense - the way people treated me, the way relatives looked out for me, the special relationship I had with my aunt (who I found out later was really my mother)."   *Adoptee*

Adoptees need some time to integrate the information that they are adopted. Questions and feelings will arise at the time of being told and throughout life. Being told that one is adopted is not necessarily a difficult time for the adoptee. On some level, adoptees know they are adopted - they were there. Being told that one is adopted merely validates their experience.

"I found out I was adopted when I was fifty years old. My mother was dying and I was going through some legal papers to get her affairs in order. I ran across my adoption papers and was shocked beyond belief. I confronted my mother on her deathbed and she finally said yes, they had adopted me. When I asked her why she hadn't told me she said there was just never a good time."   Adoptee

Some adoptees are not told they are adopted until later in life. The shock of learning this information as an adult can be overwhelming and disturbing. Most adoptees are filled with disbelief and anger at not being told the truth earlier. But they also feel a sense of relief when they learn the truth because their life makes more sense.

Any secret has the potential to cause harm and hurt feelings. It takes a lot of energy to keep secrets - to remember who knows, and who does not, and to try to figure out what to say to cover up the secret. Secrets block open communication and create feelings of mistrust between people and in families. The truth really does set one free.

Focus on Sex
"My birth mother and I don't talk about my birth father in front of her current husband. I guess it's because I'm proof that she had sex with someone else."   Adoptee

"Every time I deal with being a birth mother, I have to deal with how I got pregnant. I know a lot of other birth mothers who feel guilty for having sex and getting pregnant. Do married people who get pregnant feel guilty too? I doubt it! Isn't it funny that I did the same thing as another woman but she gets congratulated for being pregnant while I got scorn for the very same act. I guess it's just a part of being a birth mother."   Birth parent

"There's nothing like going through infertility treatment to put a damper on your sex life!"   Adoptive parent

In adoption, sex becomes a focus. A birth mother had sex and got pregnant, the adoptee is a product of sex, and the adoptive parents were having sex so they could get pregnant. In non-adoptive families, the same things can be going on but no one pays attention to them. Perhaps it is important to remember that adoptees are not the only people in the world who were unplanned pregnancies.

Needing to Blame

"I'm angry at her adoptive parents for being scared and never wanting to have anything to do with me. For turning her against me. I know their influence on her must be very strong."
          Birth parent

People typically blame others when they feel helpless, out of control, and scared. Blaming is an important part of moving through the feelings that arise in adoption. Blaming can be a way of dealing with the anger that is part of the grieving process. Sometimes other triad members are the targets of blame until the person is able to take on the responsibility of his or her own feelings.

"I was angry at my adoptive parents for a lot of years. I blamed them for everything and especially for not understanding my pain. Now I can see that they were just doing the best they could.. Looking back, I know that I needed to blame them

because being angry at them protected me from the depth of my
hurt about being abandoned by my birth mother."   *Adoptee*

The structure of adoption creates a fertile atmosphere for blaming. Continuing to blame leads to unresolved anger that builds and grows and isolates people. It is important to move through blaming to a place of understanding and responsibility. Taking responsibility involves courage, awareness, and the ability to tolerate uncomfortable feelings within one's self.

Shifting Birth Order

"My sister, an only child."   *Adoptee*

"I now talk about my son as my second first child. He was the
first son I raised but the second child I gave birth to."
                                                 Birth parent

Life is not always what it seems, and this can be particularly true in adoption. Depending on the amount of secrecy around an adoption, a person's birth order can shift dramatically and quickly. Figuring out family relationships in adoption can be especially challenging.

"I'm the youngest in my adoptive family but the oldest in my
birth family."   *Adoptee*

"It was really strange to all of a sudden have an older brother.
I guess I had always liked being the oldest in the family. I feel
as if I have lost my place in a way."
                              Biological brother of an adoptee

The birth order for an adoptee or child of a birth parent can shift at a moment's notice. This shift can feel exciting, disconcerting, and displacing. People become accustomed to filling a certain role in the family - the baby, the oldest, the middle child. It can take time to get comfortable with new family members and new family positions.

Dualities of Adoption

"I have always known that I was adopted - even before I knew what adoption was. My parents explained to me that my birth mother was unable to provide the life she wanted for me due to her age, marital status, etc., and decided to give me up for adoption. I have always felt comfortable with this, although I remember being very shy about telling my friends my adoptive status until after high school."   Adoptee

"How will my son believe that I gave him up because I loved him?"   Birth parent

"I can't imagine life without Jamie, yet I still can cry when I see a woman who is pregnant."   Adoptive parent

Adoption is filled with dualities. Adoptees are chosen while being rejected. Birth parents walk away from their children because they love them. Adoptive parents believe that adoption is positive while they mourn the possibility of biological children. The emotional feelings and issues in adoption are ever present and constantly reveal themselves. Resolving the dualities of adoption would be impossible. The best goal in dealing with these dualities is to acknowledge them and integrate them into one's life.

To Love/To Let Go

"At the home for unwed mothers, I was assigned a counselor and a social worker. The one thing that stands out in my mind is repeatedly being asked if I wanted to do the best thing for my baby. If I really loved my daughter, they said, I would let her go. Of course, I wanted to do what was best for her because I loved her with all my heart."   Birth parent

"I'm not sure exactly when it dawned on me that loving meant leaving but I do remember being told that my biological mother

*loved me so much that she decided to give me up for adoption.
When I was little, I had a completely different understanding of
what that meant. Now, as an adult, it means that it's not safe to
love anyone because they could leave too."* Adoptee

One of the dualities of adoption is the declaration that
loving means letting go. Women considering adoption are
told that if they really love their child, they will release
them for adoption. Adoptees are told that their birth
mothers loved them so much that they gave them up for
adoption. Logically, it does not make any sense to believe
that if you really love someone, you will stop having a
relationship with them. Emotionally, it is what people need
to believe to participate in adoption. It becomes clear why
love and abandonment can be so closely tied for triad
members.

Chosen/Rejected

*"We as adopted children are special - we are chosen, not just
born. Our adoptive parents had a choice. When I was in
elementary school children picked on me because I was different
- in my mind, I was special. Needless to say, I was never in the
'in' crowd. It took me a long time to develop a strong self-
esteem."* Adoptee

Adoptees in the past were often told some version of the
"chosen child story" by their adoptive parents. This story
was told to adopted children to help them feel more
comfortable with the facts of their adoption. The chosen
child story tells the child that their adoptive parents chose
them out of many different babies who were available. It
was meant to make the child feel special.

*"I laugh now when I think of how I reacted to the chosen child
story when I was a kid. I felt really special and better than the
other kids at school. It was when I was older that it occurred to*

me that if my adoptive parents chose me, then my birth mother
must have rejected me."   *Adoptee*

Usually at some point in the adoptee's life, there is the realization that being chosen has a flip side. To be chosen by the adoptive parents also means that the birth parents chose not to keep the adoptee. For many adoptees, this can feel like rejection. Not only is this duality difficult for the adoptee to understand it is also difficult for the adoptive parent to explain.

Truth/Lies

"My adoptive parents always told me that I was adopted and
that I was special. But my mother told me that I shouldn't tell
anybody about it."   *Adoptee*

Truth and deception are close neighbors in adoption. What is acceptable to talk about within the family may not be considered acceptable to talk about outside the family. Both adoptive and birth families face the task of dealing with how honest they will be about the adoption and the pregnancy. In some families, the pregnancy or adoption is not mentioned after the adoption is completed. In other families, it is unclear or unstated just what will be said. However, lies grow in the space that lacks honesty.

"My social worker promised me that I would forget my daughter
and that my life would be normal after I gave her up. I believed
what she said and thought that I could get on with my life and
that my child would be better off without me."   *Birth parent*

"We weren't told much of anything about the biological parents
when we first applied to the agency. Just the basic information
about age, interests, and marital status. We were really
surprised when we went back to the agency later and saw how
much information was there the whole time but no one had told
us."   *Adoptive parent*

Some people feel they were told untruths or lies by omission during the adoption process. Prospective adoptive parents and birth parents may not know what questions to ask and therefore depend on professionals to lead them in the right direction. The structure of adoption can hinder truth telling in a situation where honesty is crucial for the well-being of all involved.

Reality/Fantasy

"My adoptive parents never told me anything about my birth parents, so I fantasized that my father was a doctor and my mother was a prostitute. I carried this image in my mind until I received my non-identifying information at age thirty-six."

Adoptee

People automatically try to piece a picture together or draw a conclusion from the information at hand. If pieces are missing, they will seek or create replacement pieces. If reality is not available, fantasy will take its place.

"My adoptive parents told me that my birth mother had been an art student. Going to art galleries became almost an obsession for me. I kept wondering if her work was being shown."

Adoptee

"I was told that my daughter had gone to a home where there were no other children and that the parents had wanted a child for many years. I really liked holding on to this image of my daughter having a happy life with people who loved her."

Birth parent

It is not unusual for triad members to cherish the pieces of reality that they do have. Something, no matter how small or seemingly insignificant, is better than nothing at all.

6: Adoptees

"I used to say that a strong wind could blow me away because I hadn't anything tying me down. Even branches on trees have a base that can be traced back to roots beneath the ground. Even rivers can be traced back to their original banks and mouths. Adoptees, including me, are treated as if we never had umbilical cords, and yet, somehow we were born."   Adoptee

Connecting

"As a child, I always felt left out and different, as if I didn't belong. I wasn't connected to anything or anybody and I wanted to know who my birth parents were. It was hard going forward in life when I didn't know my past. I had a longing inside to know who I really was."   Adoptee

The emotional task for adoptees is to connect. Connecting involves reaching out to others, making contact, and trusting that a relationship will endure. Some adoptees are aware of feeling disconnected while others are not. Relationships can be difficult for adoptees for many different reasons.

"It took me years to come out of my shell. I meet people well, I've always worked with the public, but I make sure no one gets too close. The closest I've ever come to anyone is another adoptee. Strange, but I never get beyond that horrible barrier I've set up and probably never will. The hurt goes too deep, too long."   Adoptee

There are various levels of connecting with people. It is typically the more intimate level of relationship that is difficult for adoptees. These deeper levels of relating to others involve trust and revealing one's emotions.

Trust

"I was born and abandoned, all in one day."   *Adoptee*

"It's no wonder I became a loner. Even now, I don't trust anyone enough to get close. It's sad."   *Adoptee*

In adoption, adoptees are typically separated from the birth mother immediately or soon after birth. This is the developmental stage of learning to trust. When an infant is separated from the only mother it has known for nine months, it is more difficult for that child to establish trust. Some adoptees continue to have a difficult time in relationships. Their fear of rejection and lack of trust affects how they relate to others.

Separation of Child and Mother

"I didn't realize how sad I would be at the hospital. The adoption seemed to be the best thing, but I just couldn't stop crying when I saw my daughter. I guess the reality set in that she was a real person and I was not going to raise her."

Birth parent

"I've done some therapy where I went back to my birth experience. It was really painful for me. I kept crying and wanting my mother, but she wasn't there. I felt really alone and scared."   *Adoptee*

Separating a child and mother at birth does not go unnoticed by the mother or the child. An infant can pick out its mother from other mothers by using its senses, which have been developing and functioning in the womb. Mothers can distinguish their baby's cries from those of other babies and can begin lactating by just thinking about their child.

"The doctor gave me something to stop my milk production, but he couldn't take away my loving thoughts about the daughter I would never again see."   *Birth parent*

It is unrealistic to think that the natural experiences between a mother and her child will stop just because an adoption will take place. To assume that adoption stops these normal behaviors and emotions is to put unrealistic demands on *all* triad members.

Adapting to a New Environment

"My mother told me that I was sick for a few months when they first adopted me. They couldn't figure out what was wrong."

Adoptee

It is important for adoptive parents to know that a child recently separated from its birth parent, no matter what the reason, will be affected. The reactions may take a variety of forms and may change over time. An infant or child newly placed in an unfamiliar environment with unfamiliar people will need time to adjust to the new situation.

Being Told

"I always knew I was adopted. I guess my parents told me when I was four or five. I think at the time I didn't think much of it. It was just something that was a part of my life." *Adoptee*

"The hardest thing for me was telling him he was adopted. I didn't want him to feel bad about it. I thought we would have this sort of formal conversation about it when he was five or so. Actually, the subject came up when we were in the car so we talked about it then. I think it was harder for me than it was for him!" *Adoptive parent*

Most adoptees are told they are adopted before they reach the age of ten. This is one of the areas that adoptive parents fear most - how to tell the child, and what to tell. Adoptive parents may find it reassuring to realize that on some level, adoptees already know they were adopted - they were there.

Kids Can Be Cruel

"There was one time when being adopted hurt me the most. It was when a friend and I got into an argument and she said, 'At least I know who my real mother is!' She apologized for saying it and said she didn't mean it, but it still hurt that she used the fact that I was adopted against me."   Adoptee

Assumptions about adoption and taunts from children are still common in today's schools.   Some adoptees clearly remember being teased in school about being adopted. Sometimes non-adopted people will tell adoptees that as children they too felt that they were adopted. This is meant to make the adoptee feel better about being adopted. The difference is that for adoptees, adoption is a reality.

Finding Out Later in Life

"When I was twenty-four, I was talking with my aunt about the marital problems I was having with my husband. My aunt told me that my mother had had a hysterectomy two years before I was born. It took a while for this information to sink in. I finally realized that my aunt was telling me that I was adopted. I went through about a year of amnesia. I couldn't remember when my birthday was without looking at my driver's license. I couldn't believe my mother had never told me."   Adoptee

What could be more unsettling than finding out later in life that the basic facts of your existence are false? People feel shocked, deceived, lied to, and angry when they are not told the truth about who they are and where they come from. Telling a child the truth about his or her adoption allows the information to be integrated, embraced, and normalized.

Feeling Unwanted

"I feel sad for adoptees. I feel sad for dogs in the pound too. We are the unwanted. No matter how much our new family wants us, there is still that nagging knowledge that somewhere, someone, for some reason, didn't."   Adoptee

Many adoptees describe a feeling of being unwanted. It is easy to see where this feeling comes from because adoptees have the reality of having been let go. This feeling is separate from the love and caring that an adoptive family will provide. It is also separate from the loving feelings a birth parent may have had for their child. Feeling unwanted is an underlying feeling that will come and go at various times in an adoptee's life. It may arise when an adoptee realizes that being chosen also means being rejected or when an adoptee thinks about the relinquishment.

Abandonment and Rejection

"As an adoptee, I am constantly dealing with abandonment issues, rejection issues, and connection issues. I live with a constant feeling that I don't really belong here, like I don't really have a right to be on the planet. It feels as if everyone else is supposed to be here, but I'm a mistake. It's an unconscious feeling I've lived with all my life. Without my knowledge or permission, this feeling permeates all of my relationships and every situation."   *Adoptee*

Adoptees are familiar with the feelings of abandonment and rejection. For some adoptees, these issues are constantly present and prevent adoptees from becoming involved in relationships. For other adoptees, the fear of abandonment and rejection is never far away and can interfere with getting close to people.

"I tend to reject people before they can reject me. I have a hard time dealing with loss, abandonment, and endings, although I've gotten a lot better over the years."   *Adoptee*

Some adoptees protect themselves from the threat of rejection and abandonment by rejecting others before they can be rejected. Because every relationship has the potential for rejection and abandonment, adoptees must make a conscious effort to allow themselves to get close to people and allow intimacy. It takes time and trust for an adoptee to believe that the other person will still be there and not leave.

Outer Space
"I always describe myself as being a lost star, trying to find a similar planet to land upon."   Adoptee

Many adoptees describe feeling as if they are from outer space or from another planet. Since adoptees do not have the usual information other people have about their family history, they can feel as if they were "dropped from outer space." There is no sense of consistency over time and generations for adoptees.

"Sometimes when I see a striking resemblance between family members, I feel a slight pang of regret. I don't know anybody who looks like me."   Adoptee

Part of the sense of being from outer space is not knowing anyone who looks like you. A lack of physical similarities reminds adoptees that they are alone in the world. An adoptee's history begins with the adoptee.

Relationships
"It's gotten to the point to where I just don't have close relationships now. I hang out with some people from work but most of the time I'm by myself. I just feel more comfortable being alone. Sometimes I get sad and wish I had a girlfriend, but that feels like it would be too much work."   Adoptee

Relationships can be a struggle for adoptees. Some adoptees keep trying to connect with people and have relationships of varying degrees of closeness. Other adoptees stay within their comfort zone of closeness and prefer to spend time alone.

"I have found that in all my relationships I've pushed the woman away in a subconscious attempt to show my birth mother (by using my current partner) how it felt to be abandoned and how it felt not to be committed to the relationship."   Adoptee

Relationships can also be a struggle for the significant others in an adoptee's life. Adoptees can "test" people by pushing them away and seeing if they come back, thereby proving that they truly love the adoptee. Perhaps the adoptee is trying to master the old experience of being rejected by the birth mother by being the rejecting one in current relationships.

Being Alone
"My favorite place to be is in the car driving alone. No one can bother me; no one expects anything of me. Sometimes it feels like the only place where I can truly be me."   Adoptee

Some adoptees describe being alone as a safe place for them. When adoptees are alone, they feel there are no expectations or demands on them. For adoptees who feel they have to act or be a certain way to receive love or approval, being alone can feel like a safe haven where they can truly be themselves.

True Self/False Self
"I have always been a people pleaser and did whatever it took not to be rejected or criticized. As a youth, I always felt like a chameleon. I would try to adapt to everyone and do what I thought they wanted from me so I would be accepted and approved of."   Adoptee

Many adoptees report having difficulty knowing who they really are. They feel that they have formed themselves around the people who had expectations of them, and have tried to follow some unstated rules about who they should be and how they should behave. The fear of rejection and disapproval can force adoptees to create a false self that is the public face and persona they show to others. The true self is the authentic personality. Adoptees may have difficulty knowing their true self and may feel more comfortable being the familiar false self.

Identity Issues

"I know my identity crisis began around the time I was sixteen years old. I have always felt different, and I suppose it was because I was told that I was special and chosen. I was told that being adopted meant I was picked from all the others in the nursery. I'm now searching for my birth mother so I can find out who I am."   *Adoptee*

"I keep looking in the mirror and hoping that I'll look like someone I know."   *Adoptee*

"When I was a teenager, I kept trying to find a group to fit into. Who was I? Who was like me? Looking back, I now know that I was really needing that biological piece that was missing."
                                                              Adoptee

It is obvious that identity will be an issue for adoptees. If you don't know where you come from or who you are biologically related to, it is difficult to know who you are. Adoptive parents are an important part of an adoptee's identity but they are not the whole picture. Biological beginnings determine a great deal about who a person is.

Repeating the Pattern

"I was so sad when my daughter told me that she too had gotten pregnant and given her child up for adoption. I was sad for her, sad for her child, and sad that the pattern had repeated itself. I went through so much when I surrendered my daughter. I wouldn't wish that on anyone, especially not my daughter or grandchild."   Birth parent

Patterns can repeat themselves in families. It is not unusual for adoptees to get pregnant at around the same age that their birth mother got pregnant with them. It is important to be aware of the possibility of this pattern so that adoptees will be conscious of their actions and the potential impact.

"When I was dating, I would tell my dates that nothing was going to happen sexually for two reasons: one, that I wasn't going to have a child out of wedlock, and two, that I was scared to be sexually active with a relative I didn't know. I asked my husband a lot of questions when we dated, such as where did he live, was he adopted, etc., to make sure it wasn't possible."
                                                                  Adoptee

Some adoptees make a concerted effort to not get pregnant, imagining what their birth mothers went through and knowing what their experiences have been as an adoptee. Adoptees may also worry about whether they are dating or marrying a possible relative.

Relationship with Adoptive Parents

"Being adopted never bothered me much because I knew I had a family that loved me and cared for me and that was a lot more than most people could say."   *Adoptee*

"I have a special bond with my adoptive parents - my biological parents missed out on that. I'm forty-one years old and still live at home with them."   *Adoptee*

"I did not have a happy childhood - though it would kill my adoptive mother to hear me say that! My adoptive father beat me and emotionally abused me. I was a wreck. I tried to commit suicide, was anorexic, and became pregnant out of wedlock at age seventeen."   Adoptee

The relationships that adoptees have with their adoptive parents vary. Some adoptees feel very connected to their adoptive parents and cannot imagine being raised by anyone else. Other adoptees describe a sense of not belonging in their adoptive family. Some adoptees have had abusive experiences in their adoptive homes.

Relationship with Non-Adopted Siblings

"My sister is lucky in the sense that she knows who she resembles. She looks like my parents and when we compare her to old photos of my father's mother, there is no doubt in anyone's mind that she belongs in the family. My brothers and I look so vastly different from each other and the rest of our family that there is no doubt we were adopted. We couldn't help but to be jealous of our natural sister, because the treatment she receives in the family has always been different."   Adoptee

Adoptees raised in a family with non-adopted siblings can feel a stronger sense of not belonging in the family. The adoptee can feel that the non-adopted brother or sister gets special treatment or that the parents care more for the non-adopted sibling. There can be a sense of "us" and "them" in families with adopted and non-adopted siblings.

Fears

"I believe that the ground I walk on is the only stability I have in my life, which makes earthquakes even more frightening."
                                                         Adoptee

"Good-byes are still hard for me. I know it sounds stupid, but every time my husband goes out of town I worry that he won't come back - that something will happen to him." Adoptee

It is not unusual for adoptees to have fears that are more intense than non-adoptees. As children, adoptees may have more difficulty with times of separation such as going to sleep or the first day of school. Adult adoptees sometimes expect the worst in situations, perhaps preparing themselves in case something bad should happen. But the adoptee's reality is that fearful things, such as the original separation from the birth mother, do happen.

Daze/Numbing
"Most of the time I feel as if I move around my life in a daze. It's kind of like a fog. I like it." Adoptee

Some adoptees describe feeling as if they are in a daze or numbed out. This numbing can be seen as a defense against dealing with difficult information and feelings. Many adoptees would be too overwhelmed by the reality of their situation if they experienced total clarity. Instead, living with fogginess feels comforting and protective. To have clarity is a challenge for many people. For adoptees, certain feelings may be too intense to confront.

Post Traumatic Stress Disorder
"When I think about it, I can't really imagine how it was for me to be separated from my birth mother. She was the only one who was familiar to me." Adoptee

Post Traumatic Stress Disorder (PTSD) is a condition that often affects people who have experienced a traumatic event that is considered outside the range of normal human experience such as rape, fires, earthquakes, and tornadoes.

The separation of a child from its mother is also a trauma that is outside the range of normal human experience.

"No wonder I always get sad around my birthday. That is the day my world changed."   *Adoptee*

"My parents would always try to make my birthday a celebration and throw a big party. I really tried to be in a party mood but it was hard. There was this sadness that I just couldn't shake."   *Adoptee*

PTSD symptoms can include trying to avoid situations that remind the person of the traumatic event, having flashback memories, and anniversary reactions. It can be said that an adoptee's birthday is the anniversary of a traumatic event. Some adoptees feel sad around their birthdays or remember birthdays as a time when they acted out or got in trouble.

Difficult Beginnings

"I was born in a psychiatric hospital. My birth mother had been hospitalized there for manic depression for six months before my birth. I stayed with her for six weeks and then went into about six different foster homes."   *Adoptee*

Some adoptees' beginnings are even more difficult. Having a birth mother with a mental illness or moving through foster homes will have an impact on the adoptee. Infants and children need security, consistency, and people they can depend on.

Adoptee as Survivor

"Having been an orphan and growing up with a lot of responsibility has made me an extremely independent and strong person. Surprisingly, I have fairly good self-esteem but I think it took a lot of work."   *Adoptee*

"I never doubt my ability to survive. I got through this adoption thing, and I'll get through anything else. I'm not glad I was adopted, but I know I am a much stronger person for it."

Adoptee

Adoptees have, by the very act of adoption, gone through a lot. By the time adoptees are adults, they have survived separation from their birth parents, have acclimated to a new family, have dealt with fantasy and fears, have confronted identity issues, and have navigated many relationships. Being an adoptee means moving through some difficult stages and transitions. The awareness of having survived can give adoptees strength and determination in various areas of their lives. The downside of this feeling of survival is that some adoptees find it difficult to depend on others and instead are very independent. It is important for adoptees to realize that healthy relationships involve interdependence - depending on one's self and depending on others.

Denial

"I was very reluctant to search until I was thirty-six years old. I always said that I didn't want to find my birth parents and that I wasn't interested in them. In reality, the fear of rejection kept me from searching."

Adoptee

Some adoptees state that they have no interest in meeting or knowing about their birth families. This denial can be a protection against all the feelings that could arise if the adoptee "opened that can of worms." Denial is a natural way of shutting down in a situation that feels overwhelming.

"The question is not 'How can someone be interested in finding out who they are?' The question is 'How can someone not be interested in finding out who they are?'"

Adoptee

Most adoptees pass through a period of denying interest in their birth family at some point in their lives. A dawning awareness of the issues and feelings surrounding adoption can break through this denial and lead the adoptee to question various aspects of his or her own history and of adoption itself.

Triggers

"Doing a family tree in school was very hard for me. It felt like a lie, or at least not the whole truth. Kids would say they were Irish or German, and I didn't have a clue."   Adoptee

"I still look in the mirror and wonder who I resemble. People comment that I look so much younger than my chronological age and that I should be thankful to have gotten such wonderful genes. To some this may sound like a compliment. To me, it sounds painful because I haven't a clue as to where I got these genes. I don't have anyone to thank."   Adoptee

"There were moments that I wished I knew my birth mother, especially when the song 'Somewhere Out There' came on the radio. Every time that song played, I would sing along and start crying because I wanted to meet her so much."   Adoptee

Seemingly simple questions, comments, or situations can trigger emotions for adoptees. A family tree school assignment will be challenging for an adoptee. Being asked if cancer runs in your family may make an adoptee sad because they don't know the answer. Even looking in the mirror can create questions for adoptees. Questions that most people answer without thinking can raise many difficult issues for adoptees.

7: Birth Parents

"I wouldn't wish being a birth mother on anyone." Birth parent

Birth Mothers

"I was told that a seventeen-year-old couldn't care or provide for a child. I was told that every child needs two parents. I was told that if I did not sign the papers I would live on the streets with my daughter. My parents told me I couldn't bring her home. I was told that I'd go on and forget her, marry, and have other children. I was told that I was doing the right thing for my daughter and myself. But I was also told to never ever tell anyone about what had happened to me because people might look down on me."
Birth parent

A pregnant woman becomes a birth mother after she gives birth to her child and agrees to an adoption plan. She signs a legal document that terminates her parental rights to that child. For many birth mothers, the entire experience from conception to pregnancy to adoption and beyond is emotional, overwhelming, confusing, and unforgettable.

"We are misunderstood, blamed, and considered to be people of low moral character. What people don't understand is that we were dying inside when we gave our babies up for adoption. We didn't want to, but we didn't feel like we had any other choice. No one supported our wanting to keep our children."
Birth parent

Birth mothers typically have memories and feelings about their entire experience. Being pregnant, considering options, getting or not getting support from others, the relinquishment, and the aftereffects of the adoption are all momentous occasions for birth mothers. For many birth mothers, signing the adoption papers does not signify the end of their adoption experience but rather marks the beginning of a whole new phase.

"My memories about that time in my life are pretty cloudy. I remember finding out I was pregnant and being so afraid of what my parents would say. I hoped it would just go away. When it didn't go away, I told my parents and they sort of took care of everything - calling the agency and setting up appointments. I remember crying a lot then. It was only later that I was able to get angry too."   Birth mother

Any woman who goes through a pregnancy and then relinquishes her child would be expected to have strong feelings about the experience. Some women are immediately aware of their feelings at the time, while others shut down emotionally to protect themselves from the intensity of their feelings. Sometimes it takes years for birth mothers to realize the full extent of their feelings about the adoption.

Birth Fathers
"It sure was a surprise to me to find out that I had a twenty-five-year- old daughter! I guess that if I had been told at the time it would be different. It's taking some getting used to. Maybe I'm still in shock."   Birth father

Birth fathers are perhaps the most forgotten part of the adoption triad. Some birth fathers were never told of the pregnancy. Other birth fathers are told that they cannot take part in the planning for the future of their child. Some birth fathers leave of their own accord because they don't want to deal with the situation.

"I don't think people realize that birth fathers suffer too. When I go to support group meetings, I feel like I am blamed for every birth father who didn't care about his child. But I did care, and

I was there. I lost my first child too. There's nothing I can do to change that now, but I still think about it a lot. No one really asked me what I wanted. We were just told what we had to do."
Birth father

Birth fathers can have strong feelings about the adoption of their child. Birth fathers and birth mothers are forever linked to their children. Adoption does not erase this fact.

"When I was ten years old, my adoptive mother told me that my birth father had died. I broke down in tears. She asked me why I was crying for somebody I didn't know. I replied, 'Because now I'll never know him.'"
Adoptee

The loss of the birth father will be felt by the adoptee. It is difficult to disregard half of who you are. Adoptees who want to know where they come from know that they had two birth parents and that both contributed in their own way.

"In 1968, I found myself pregnant and went to my child's father to tell him. Two days later, he was gone from our lives. He went into the service and off to Vietnam. I've never seen him since."
Birth parent

Some circumstances keep birth fathers away from their children and from taking part in planning for the child's life. Every effort must be made to include each parent when making major decisions. Acknowledging and expecting both parents to be a part of a child's life is positive because it means that they are coming together for the sake of the child.

Birth Mother/Birth Father Relationship
"He was my first love. We met in high school and dated for two years. We had plans to get married and have a family.

Unfortunately, I got pregnant, and it turned our whole world upside down. We wanted to get married, but our parents thought we should break up and give the baby up for adoption. That was the hardest time of my life. We never really were able to get past all that happened. He went away to school and I didn't see him or talk to him for five years."   Birth mother

The kind of relationship that the birth mother and birth father have affects the process of adoption and the feelings connected with the crisis in their lives. Sometimes the losses of adoption are magnified by the additional loss of the birth mother and birth father relationship.

"He was someone I barely knew. When I found out I was pregnant, I went back to where he worked to tell him. They said he had moved to Oregon. I've never seen him since. I'd like to know where he is now because I want to tell him that he has a beautiful daughter. I'm sure he has no idea."   Birth parent

Sometimes the relationship between the birth mother and the birth father is distant, or there is no further communication between the two. This additional loss of connection and support will affect the adoption and future feelings about the time surrounding the adoption.

Forgiveness

"I've waited so long for my daughter to forgive me. After we met, I knew that it wasn't up to her. I needed to forgive myself. Through meditation and visualizations, I opened my heart and forgave myself. With her latest outburst, I didn't feel guilty. Perhaps that's why there was room for me to be angry. It is a step up from depression."   Birth parent

The task for birth parents is to forgive themselves. Many birth parents carry the burden of blame and guilt around for years. Some birth parents want forgiveness from the adoptee, their family, or society. To forgive oneself is a gift that every birth parent deserves and can learn to do.

"I have realized over the years that my mother was only doing what she thought was best for my daughter and myself. The daughter I released was the only granddaughter my mother ever had. And she never got to know her." Birth parent

Forgiveness can also extend to the people who were in the birth parent's life at the time of the pregnancy and relinquishment. Most likely, everyone involved was doing what they felt was best at the time.

"I know my son doesn't really understand what it was like for me when I was pregnant in 1960. There wasn't any welfare available for me, and women who weren't married did not keep their babies. There weren't the choices that there are today."
Birth parent

It is important to remember that birth parents today have choices that were not available in the past. Society has changed in many ways that have opened up options and choices. Acknowledging the differences in time and attitudes from the past to the present can accelerate forgiveness.

Shame

"Due to her shame, my birth mother couldn't tell my half-brother and sister about me for ten years. My birth father has still not told his wife or two sons about me." Adoptee

Shame is a feeling that can paralyze people and cause people to hide the truth. Shame is the feeling that you have done something wrong and that people will think badly of you. In adoption, shame can last for years beyond the actual time of the adoption. Some birth parents, because of their shame, have never told anyone about their adoption experience.

Guilt

"Having sex was not my choice. It was a terrible experience. I remember sobbing and crying and asking my boyfriend to stop. I know I was starting to feel a lot more for him than I wanted to, but I was not ready for sex. I know I am not blameless. I should have stopped him before it got out of control."   Birth parent

Guilt is a common feeling for a birth parent to carry around. There can be guilt about having sex, guilt about getting pregnant, and guilt about deciding on adoption. Guilt feelings can mean that the person has not yet forgiven himself or herself for behaviors or events of the past. However, if people can realize that they can do nothing about a situation, they may then be able to release their guilt.

Relief

"There was a feeling of relief when I finally decided on an adoption plan. I felt bad that I couldn't keep my baby, but I knew that a baby would be better off with parents who could take care of it. I couldn't. I was glad that there were people who could raise my child in a proper way."   Birth parent

There can be a sense of relief when birth parents decide that adoption is the best option. The decision to choose adoption is usually reached after all the other options have been considered. This is not to say that other emotions will not also be present or arise later.

Anger

"Separating a mother and her child has got to be the most inhumane and cruel form of punishment known to mankind. I would have preferred execution!"   Birth parent

Birth parents can become angry at some point in their lives about their experience with the adoption process. For some birth parents, this anger is present during the decision to relinquish, while for others the anger comes years later. Anger is an emotion that naturally occurs when there is loss or a feeling of being out of control. Anger can also motivate people to actions such as searching for their child or fighting for adoption reform.

Sadness

"I have become painfully aware that I am not over the adoption yet. Twelve years of tears and I am hopefully on the path to healing. At my first support group meeting, I burst into tears as soon as I left. It was the same guttural cry I cried when I lost Matthew." Birth parent

A birth parent's sadness can seem to take on a life of its own. There are no time limits to mourning the loss of a child. The depth of their sadness surprises some birth parents so long after the relinquishment. It is best to acknowledge this sadness, let oneself feel it, and know that people don't get more than they can handle. All feelings pass.

Depression

"In the first few months after the relinquishment, I honestly thought I was losing my mind. After all, I was told that I would forget this baby and go on with my life as though she never existed! Well, I was not forgetting. The pain intensified and I became extremely depressed. I really felt that I wanted to die. I recall falling to pieces every time I saw a baby my daughter's age. Could she be mine?" Birth parent

Depression is a feeling of hopelessness and helplessness. There is a sense that things will never change and that there will not be brighter days ahead. It is natural to feel depressed after a loss. Losing a child is a major loss in a parent's life. Birth parents will feel this loss in one way or another.

Relationships

"I have realized that this whole experience has caused me problems with trust in my marriage and with friendships. I have suffered from low self-esteem, depression, and guilt and shame. I am working really hard to try to overcome the old me."

Birth parent

Being a birth parent has an impact on relationships. The low self-esteem that many birth parents describe can get in the way of their starting and keeping relationships. Birth parents sometimes find it hard to believe that someone could truly care about them and love them. Trusting others can also be a stumbling block.

"I got a job, then joined the service, traveled, saw the world, and slowly began healing. I told anyone who wanted to know that I was a birth mother. I was not ashamed of bringing David into this world. I got out of the service, went home, tried to find permanent, steady work. It didn't happen. I finally got a job in the Midwest. I thought I was somewhat healed, but I was wrong. I had never formed a permanent bond with another man. I came close once, even got engaged, but that did not work out. So I decided that I would never marry. It was in the cards, so to speak."   *Birth parent*

Some birth parents feel doomed to failure because of their experience in having gone through the process of pregnancy, deciding on adoption, and the relinquishment. Future relationships will be affected by how the birth parent views himself or herself in terms of the adoption process.

Sexuality

"There's a part of me that still has a difficult time enjoying sex. I feel as if I should still be paying my dues for getting pregnant and giving my baby up for adoption." Birth parent

For some birth parents, sex is a reminder of the adoption experience. Acknowledging and dealing with the many feelings associated with being a birth parent can help to make sex a more enjoyable activity.

Scars

"My doctor was not a friendly man but he was, underneath, good and compassionate. I broke down while he was examining me around four or five months into the pregnancy and from that time on he treated me with respect. I made him promise not to give me a Cesarean unless absolutely necessary. I did not want to carry the scar if I had no child to show for it. He was true to his word." Birth parent

Many birth mothers carry the physical signs and scars of having given birth. Getting dressed and seeing stretch marks or a C-section scar can be a trigger to birth mothers. Deciding to have a physical relationship with someone can also prompt old feelings and force a birth mother to tell her partner about having been pregnant. To many birth mothers, these are painful reminders of a difficult time both emotionally and physically.

Role Confusion - Then and Now

"My maternal instincts were taking over. By the seventh month, when I went into the maternity home, I was feeling pretty attached to my baby. By the time she was born, I really wanted to keep her." Birth parent

A birth mother is a mother in many ways - physically, emotionally, and spiritually. Many birth mothers describe feeling very connected to their unborn child. Bonding with one's unborn child is a natural part of being pregnant. It can be confusing to feel so connected to a baby that one will not raise.

"Do I have the right to say that I have a son? He's somebody else's son. But what would I call him if not son?"   Birth parent

It can be confusing to be a parent and not a parent. Birth parents will struggle with their identity as it relates to their role as a parent. Are people still mothers or fathers if they don't raise their child?

Pregnancy = Crisis

"When I finally worked up the nerve to tell my mother about my pregnancy and our decision to marry, she refused to allow me to marry my boyfriend. She somehow managed to set up an abortion for me - although abortions were still illegal in the fall of 1969 - and tried to force me to go through with the abortion."

Birth parent

For every birth parent, pregnancy is a crisis. People in crisis often have difficulty making decisions, may find that their moods shift easily, and may react in ways that seem unusual for them. Those around the birth parents may also be feeling the effects of the crisis and act in ways that help or hinder the situation.

Loss

"I became pregnant with my son after I was divorced from my abusive and alcoholic husband. Giving my son up for adoption was the hardest thing I have had to do in my life. I have two daughters by the same father."   Birth parent

Birth parents are not the only ones who feel the loss of adoption. Sometimes there are full siblings in a family who also lose their brother or sister to adoption. In every case, adoption is a difficult decision. When adoption involves separating more than the birth parents and child, it can feel like even more of a loss.

"I am the youngest of eight kids in my birth family. I was adopted when I was two. Before that I was in a foster home, but they couldn't adopt me because my brothers knew where I was and the foster parents were afraid that they would come and kidnap me and take me back. My adoptive mother told me that me and my two sisters were taken away because my dad was a bad man. I don't know how much of this is true. I want to find my birth family so I can learn the truth about what really happened."   *Adoptee*

Loss is loss regardless of the circumstances. Even in families where a child is taken out of the home due to abuse or neglect, the child still needs and craves an emotional connection to his or her birth family. Without the truth, many children create ideas about how things could be. These children grow into adults who continue to search for the truth and mourn what might have been had they remained with their birth family.

Pregnancy as a Result of Rape

"I became a birth mother at the age of fifteen. The son of the apartment handyman came over to fix a pipe. When I let him in, he raped me. I was in shock and afraid of what my mother would say when I told her how this boy had hurt me. When I finally got up the courage to tell her, she called me every name in the book. She thought it was my fault. When I found out I was pregnant, she sent me to another state and told me not to tell anyone."   *Birth parent*

Clearly, being pregnant as the result of a rape adds to the trauma of being pregnant. Along with the shame about being pregnant and carrying a child, the violence of the conception stays with the woman for her lifetime.

"After a long search, I found my daughter. We exchanged pictures, we met. Since she was having such a hard time dealing with our reunion, I decided to put off telling her the whole story of what happened... of her conception."   Birth parent

For any birth parent, the story of conception can be difficult. When conception involves rape, it can weigh more heavily on a birth parent's mind.

"As time has gone on, it's become more important for me to tell my daughter what really happened. I didn't want her to hear it from someone else. And I believe it is her right to know the truth. Initially I told her he was someone I knew briefly, a partial truth."   Birth parent

Birth mothers who conceived during a rape have to decide how to tell their child of the circumstances of their conception. Understandably, this piece of information is difficult for all concerned. However, as in other areas of adoption, people deserve to know the truth.

Treatment of Birth Mothers

"The adoption agency gathered information from me about my background and about the birth father's background. Yet they would not give me any clue as to who the adoptive family would be. They placed me in a home for unwed mothers and I was cut off from friends and family. I did not see my mother and stepfather until they picked me up two days after I delivered my son."   Birth parent

Many birth parents report being treated in negative ways by people during the pregnancy and the adoption process. Some birth parents were separated from their most important support system of family and friends while they were pregnant.

"I tried to stay in my room as much as possible since my mother was on me constantly whenever she saw me. She told me over and over again what an idiot I was for getting pregnant. She blamed me, my deceased father, and my boyfriend. I was reduced to tears daily. She told me what a good thing it was that I felt bad about being pregnant because I deserved to feel bad."   *Birth parent*

Some birth parents lost the support of their own family members when they became pregnant. If they had no place else to go, they stayed with their families and tried to deal with the relationships around them. It was not unusual for birth parents to be told that they deserved to be treated poorly because of what they had done to become pregnant.

Relinquishment

"I got to hold her when she was two days old, for about ten minutes. I was struck by two things - how much she looked like me and that life is a miracle!"   *Birth parent*

Relinquishment is when the birth parent releases the child for adoption. The hospital experience, childbirth, seeing the baby or not, treatment by the doctors and nurses, and the signing of the adoption papers are all a part of the relinquishment experience.

"The next day, the caseworker brought the relinquishment papers for me to sign. All night long I had lain awake trying to think of a way to get around signing those papers. I fantasized about getting dressed, finding my baby, and sneaking out of the hospital with her. Instead, I signed the papers. It was a very strange feeling. I felt almost as if I was standing across the room from myself watching myself sign them. I seemed to keep

*expecting someone or something to happen at the last minute to
stop the whole nightmare."*   *Birth parent*

Every birth mother and some birth fathers have a
relinquishment story - the details around the event of
releasing their child. When birth parents tell their story of
relinquishment, it is usually with emotion and feeling.

*"My parents said that keeping my baby girl would ruin my life
and hers. They said they would not accept a bastard grandchild.
They asked me how I could do this to them.   No one ever asked
me what this was doing to me.   No one asked me what living
without my daughter would do to me.   No one asked me if this
was what I wanted."*   *Birth parent*

For many birth parents, the relinquishment experience,
which involved dealing with parents and adoption agencies,
was a time of confusion and fear. Relinquishment is a time
when support and the level of shame in the family reveal
family dynamics.

Saying Goodbye

*"I loved her so much. I told her goodbye and how sorry I was.
It was the hardest thing I've ever done in my life. I bent down to
kiss her cheek and promised her that someday we would find
each other."*   *Birth parent*

What could be more difficult than saying goodbye to your
newborn child? Some birth parents have the opportunity to
spend time with their baby and say goodbye face-to-face.

*"I never got to see her. They said it would be better if I didn't
hold her or look at her. I didn't even know where she was in the
hospital."*   *Birth parent*

Some birth parents are not allowed to see their infant. It was typical for birth mothers to be placed in rooms on floors other than the maternity floor and to not expect to see their baby. For these birth parents, the goodbye can be more difficult. How can a person say goodbye if there has never been a hello?

Post-Relinquishment Experience

"I said goodbye to her two days before Thanksgiving. It was horrible. I felt numb, dead, blank. I didn't think I'd ever be normal again, if there was a 'normal.' To make matters worse, my parents told me that we would never mention it again. So I had no one to talk to at all."   Birth parent

Many birth parents describe feeling numb during the time period immediately after relinquishment. Post-relinquishment is a time when birth parents need to heal and recover from a traumatic experience. Support, especially from family members and friends, is crucial. To not talk about the relinquishment only postpones the healing.

"For several years after the adoption, I felt as if I was in a trance - numb by the loss and fearful that someone would find out. You see then, in 1964, it was hush-hush - don't tell anyone."   Birth parent

Adoptions of the past were more secretive than they are today. Many birth parents of the past had to live in secrecy about their pregnancy and adoption experience.

"I met a wonderful man, got married, and had two sons. But I never did forget my daughter."   Birth parent

The relinquishment experience is not forgotten. Birth parents can later get married and have more children.

However, getting married and having more children does not erase the relinquishment or adoption experience.

Post Traumatic Stress Disorder

"The doctors and counselors said I was suffering from Post Traumatic Stress Disorder. I started losing weight, had flashbacks, felt severe grief and loss feelings, couldn't sleep, and was barely making it through each day."   *Birth parent*

Post Traumatic Stress Disorder (PTSD) is a diagnosis given to people who are feeling the effects of a traumatic event that happened recently or in the past. Losing a child is a traumatic experience. It is not unusual for birth parents to experience symptoms of Post Traumatic Stress Disorder at some point after the relinquishment of their child.

Support Then and Now

"When the nurse took her away, I went down the hall to the pay phone to call my parents to see if I could bring her home. They said 'no.' That was the final nail in the coffin of my having any chance of keeping her. A great void in my heart replaced the baby I had carried for nine months."   *Birth parent*

Many birth parents looked to their parents for permission to keep their child. In the past, government assistance programs did not exist as they do today. Many birth parents were dependent on their parents for emotional and financial support, which meant that their parents were part of the adoption decision.

"I felt so lost, scared, and abandoned. I always thought my parents would be there for me and would help me through any problems I would ever have. They took the news of my pregnancy very badly and put me in a home for unwed mothers. I felt so rejected, not only by my parents but also by the birth father."   *Birth parent*

During times of crisis, people need a strong support system. Many birth parents did not have a support system of family and friends. This lack of support adds to the trauma of an unplanned pregnancy. It is sad that at a time when support is so crucial, a birth parent can feel so alone and frightened.

"I found a support group for birth parents, adoptees, and adoptive parents. For the first time in my life, I found people who I could talk to and cry with who really understood the pain." Birth parent

Some birth parents do not get the support they need until years later. Support groups offer birth parents a safe and supportive place where their feelings can be validated and they can speak honestly about their experiences.

Future Children

"I've always felt that in a way I don't deserve to have any other children. Maybe after being told so many times that I couldn't take care of that first baby, I believed that I couldn't take care of any baby. If I wasn't worthy of the first one, why should I be worthy of any others?" Birth parent

The decision to have future children can be a difficult one for birth parents. Thoughts of the child relinquished for adoption can make birth parents doubt their ability and capacity to have more children.

"I decided not to have any more children. I did not think I could bear holding another baby in my arms when my heart ached so for the little one I gave away." Birth parent

Some birth parents decide not to have more children. The fear is that future children would be a reminder of the child relinquished for adoption.

Triggers

"I can't tell you how many times people have told me that I wouldn't understand because I'm not a mother. Well, I am a mother even though I didn't raise my son!"   Birth parent

Adoption issues can be triggered on a daily basis. Everyday conversations can touch a birth parent and cause adoption related feelings to come to the surface.

"I feel a little neglected and envy women whose significant life milestones are publicly celebrated. I get uncomfortable and even resentful when co-workers celebrate their pregnancies with lots of attention from others. Meanwhile I am discounted for having the same experience because I'm not married and raising children."   Birth parent

Birth mothers do not get the public celebration that other mothers receive. It can be difficult for a birth mother to attend a baby shower or to shop for a baby gift when she feels that she didn't receive the same attention or acknowledgment.

"Every year around his birthday, I get really depressed. Now I just accept it as part of being a birth mother."   Birth parent

The birthday of a relinquished child can be a trigger time for a birth parent. It is an anniversary of a traumatic and sad event. It is not uncommon for birth parents to feel sad and depressed around their child's birthday. It is important for birth parents to take extra care of themselves during this time.

8: Adoptive Parents

"We finally have our little girl!"　　　　　*Adoptive parent*

Infertility

"We went through so much with the infertility treatments. Our lives revolved around ovulation kits and doctors' appointments. There was a point where we just had to stop the treatments and think about the alternatives. We started to explore adoption and talked to people who had gone through the process."

Adoptive parent

Infertility is one of the main reasons that people choose to adopt. People who turn towards adoption after infertility treatments have typically gone through years of trying to have a biological child and have spent much time, energy, and money in their pursuit of parenting.

Decision to Adopt

"I couldn't imagine <u>not</u> being a parent. Ever since I was a little girl, I wanted to be a mother. Not being able to get pregnant has been devastating for me. Now my attention is concentrated on adopting. It feels like a full-time job! I have a lot of dreams that I am needing to adjust in my life. It hasn't been easy, but I'm trying."　　　　　*Pre-adoptive parent*

"I was forty-three years old and not married. I knew I wanted to raise a child, but I didn't want to wait for a man to come into my life. And besides, having a biological child was getting very iffy at my age. I decided to adopt."　　　　　*Adoptive parent*

"We thought of all the ways we could parent a child. We considered surrogacy and decided against it. We had concerns that as a same sex couple we might have a difficult time adopting."　　　　　*Adoptive parent*

People want to parent for various reasons. The decision to adopt is a conscious decision that necessitates action and follow through. Sometimes the decision to adopt is made after an extensive period of time of wanting to raise a child. Sometimes adoption is seen as one of the few options available to be a parent.

Adoption Is a Permanent Decision

"I can't believe the comments I get from people about my son because he is in prison. They want to know if I feel relieved that he is adopted and not really mine! They don't understand that my son could not be more my son if I had given birth to him. You don't stop loving your children because of what they do. They are yours forever."   Adoptive parent

"I still feel furious at the callous way the adoptive parents dumped my son when they thought he had brain damage. Why couldn't they have at least accompanied him to the hospital to help him get settled in? They were the only parents he knew. It was heartbreaking to know that my son could not understand the desertion of people he had considered to be his mother and father."   Birth parent

Adoption should be entered into as a permanent decision. Children are not returnable. One way in which children feel secure and move beyond their separation from their birth parents is by having a safe environment and dependable people around them.

Honesty versus Secrecy

"I've been totally open with my son since the cradle. I truly believe that if a child can't trust a parent to be honest about who he is, he can't trust that parent on anything."   Adoptive parent

"I have always known I was adopted because my mother was never afraid to tell me so. She answered any question I asked as long as she knew the answer."   Adoptee

The adoptive parent is a role model for honesty in adoption. If the adoptive parent can be honest with the adoptee, the adoptee will not feel as though there is something bad to hide. Secrecy promotes low self-esteem, mistrust, and a lack of safety.

Fears

"When we started talking to birth mothers, we worried about drugs and how healthy the baby would be."   Adoptive parent

"We had heard all those horror stories on TV about the birth parents coming back to claim their child. We were worried about it, but when someone pointed out to us that those cases are rare, we were more relaxed. We realized that a birth parent having second thoughts is just a part of what's involved in the whole process of adoption."   Adoptive parent

It is natural to have fears about adoption. Some adoptive parents worry that their child will be defective in some kind of way. Some adoptive parents fear that the birth parents will change their mind. Clear communication of expectations and feelings can relieve some of the fears that surround adoption.

Whose Child?

"When I was pregnant with my son, the way I worked it out was that I didn't think 'my baby' but rather 'the baby' or 'the fetus.' I told myself that soon he will be going to his parents; I wasn't really his mother. I daresay the adoptive parents probably had the same veils to go through. It would have been so much better if we could have thought that we were all four his real parents."   Birth parent

It can be very difficult to know that you are pregnant with a child that someone else will raise. Many birth parents and adoptive parents adjust their thinking and beliefs to be able to embrace all that adoption means.

"During the time I was pregnant, I knew he was not to be my child - I was just carrying him for someone else whose child he would be. I didn't suffer the empty-arms syndrome I've heard of - women longing for their lost child. I trusted he would be well cared for, as he indeed was."   *Birth parent*

For some birth parents, knowing the prospective adoptive parents is reassuring. Other birth parents trust that whoever the adoptive parents are, they will take good care of the child. Maintaining the thought of carrying a child for other people allows the birth parent to have some emotional distance from the situation.

"Since we adopted Christine when she was two years old, we could readily accept that she had had other parents before us."
Adoptive parent

When adopting an older child, it is sometimes more obvious that the birth parents have been a part of the child's life. Regardless of the age of the adoptee at the time of adoption, there are roles and places for all the parents.

Bonding versus Attachment

"I have two very special relationships with my two mothers. I thank my birth mother for giving me life and loving me those nine months we were together. I love my adoptive mother for caring for me as only a mother could - being there when I was sick, or sad, or needed a peanut butter-and-jelly sandwich. One relationship is not better than the other or more important to me. I needed both of them."   *Adoptee*

Bonding is a biological process. It happens in utero between a pregnant woman and her unborn child. Attachment occurs after birth and outside the womb. Birth mothers bond with their babies. Adoptive parents form attachments to their infants and children. Each relationship is crucial to the well-being of the adoptee.

Loving Your Child

"I can't imagine my life without our son. From the moment I learned I was 'going to have a baby' until now, twenty-five years later, I smile at the thought. If he did not grow within me, you could never tell. One ceases to think of how he got here, because he is undeniably yours in every way but blood."

Adoptive parent

"I couldn't love this child any more than if I had given birth to her. We fell in love with her the moment we laid our eyes on her. That first smile melted us."   *Adoptive parent*

Adoptive parents do not love their children any less than non-adoptive parents. Most adoptive parents state that the minute they saw their child they loved him or her. Adoptive parents love their children as any parent does.

Role as Parent

"My adoptive mother, who died after a long illness last year, was my best friend. I could not have asked for a better mother. I feel that she was infertile so that she could adopt me and I feel that my birth mother got pregnant unexpectedly because I was to be her gift to someone else, my mother. I consider myself to be rather lucky."   *Adoptee*

An adoptive parent is no less a parent than a biological parent. Adoptees love their adoptive parents as any child loves a parent. The adoptive parent's job is to raise the child, love the child, and consider the child's best interest. Adoptive parents share the role of parent with all other parents in the world.

Telling Your Child

"I was adopted as an infant. My parents told me I was adopted when I was four years old. I feel I was able to grasp the concept from what I remember. My older brother is also adopted. My oldest brother is not."   *Adoptee*

Some adoptive parents worry about how to tell their child that he or she is adopted. It is important to remember that on some level the adoptee already knows about the separation and adoption. It is usually the adoptive parents who have a difficult time with talking about adoption. Children want to know about their adoption because it is about them. All children like to hear stories about when they were babies and what they were like growing up.

"I remember when David came home from school and asked whether he had come out of my tummy. I was so startled and didn't know what to say. Was he asking about sex, or was he asking about adoption? After I took a couple of breaths, I was able to hear his questions more clearly."   *Adoptive parent*

It is important to be truthful with children and to give them enough information to answer their questions. Sometimes adoptive parents are so concerned about hurting their child by telling him or her that they are adopted that they miss the real questions being asked.

"I was in foster care for nine months before I was released for adoption. I met my adoptive family for the first time at the Howard Johnson's halfway between the foster home and my adoptive parents' home. When I was older and questioned my parents about where babies come from my father told me 'Howard Johnson's'!"   *Adoptee*

"We adopted both our children from Korea. I'll never forget when my son asked about where babies come from. I was concerned about how to tell him about his adoption. I told him all about getting on a plane and flying to Korea to pick him and his sister up. Later he told everyone at the dinner table that he was born in a plane. We laughed about it at the time, but now I realize that I didn't talk about him having other parents because it was too difficult for me to include them in his story."
          Adoptive parent

Adopted children need to know that they are born like all other children. Babies do not come from Howard Johnson's, planes, or hospitals.

Birth Mothers and Birth Fathers

"I was very aware that I started tearing up when my daughter asked about her beginnings. She seemed so interested in who the birth parents were. I wasn't sure how much to tell her, how much she could handle at her age."   Adoptive parent

Every person has a birth mother and a birth father. In adoption, caretakers other than the birth parents raise adoptees. It is important to acknowledge the role and necessity of birth parents when talking with adopted children about their origins.

"When my daughter asks about her birth parents, I don't always know what to say. I also find myself feeling bad that she wants to know about them. Does it mean that we're not enough?"

Adoptive parent

Wanting to know information about oneself is a natural curiosity. Adoptees wonder about their history and where they come from. Adoptees do not think less of their adoptive parents when they have questions about their birth parents.

Acknowledging Birth Parents

"It has taken some time, but we are now able to have a place in our hearts and minds for our daughter's birth parents. They are, after all, the reason we have her!"   Adoptive parent

"It's funny, I think I want to find my son's birth mother more than he does. I want to know who she is and to thank her for my beautiful and wonderful son. He is such a gift, and I'm sure she must wonder about him. I would love to thank her in person."

Adoptive parent

Birth parents are a part of every adoption. To deny an adoptee's birth parents is to cut off a part of the adoptee's identity. To acknowledge birth parents is to respect the adoptee's history, which is rich with the contributions of both the adoptive parents and the birth parents.

Talking about Adoption Issues

"We talk about his adoption openly (I don't think he and my husband have ever said a single word about it), and he really has no desire to search. He says, 'I am who I am, and I can live with that' so I certainly won't pursue it. Except, of course, if health problems arise and then we'll turn the world upside down to find her."   *Adoptive parent*

Some adoptees may not ask many questions about the adoption or may not act interested in knowing about the birth parents. This stance can change over time or remain the same. Talking openly about adoption issues and feelings allows the adoptee to feel free to bring up any concerns or questions he or she may have.

"There are lots of questions I have about my birth parents that I don't ask my adoptive parents. I don't want to hurt them or make them feel bad."   *Adoptee*

Many adoptees have questions about adoption that they don't ask their adoptive parents. Adoptees typically worry about hurting their adoptive parents' feelings. Openness on the part of the adoptive parents can help create an atmosphere in which adoption issues can be discussed.

Integrating Infertility and Adoption

"I can't imagine not having my boys. They have felt as if they were ours from the very beginning. Still, there have been times when I couldn't help but wonder how they would have been different if we had given birth to them."   *Adoptive parent*

"My daughter is now pregnant with her first child. I can give her love and support and I'm so happy for her, but I will never share the childbirth experience with her."   Adoptive parent

Infertility is an issue that will weave its way through the lifetime of an adoptive parent. Sometimes people are caught off guard by the timing or degree of feelings about infertility issues. Being able to acknowledge one's feelings about infertility is important.

"The first time I saw him, I felt I'd burst! And the first time I held him, I knew I was in love and bonded with him forever. You forget that you weren't pregnant (although I admit I regret I never had that experience) and instead are so grateful that someone else was and had the generosity of heart and common sense to bestow this incredible gift on you."   Adoptive parent

The losses and gains in adoption are very near to each other and sometimes acknowledging one brings up the other. Being honest about one's feelings and allowing oneself the time to feel their impact is healing.

Biological versus Adoptive Parenting

"My parents always told my brother and I that love, not biology, makes a family. But I have always been curious about my birth family. I have questions that only they can answer."   Adoptee

Love does indeed make a family. But biology matters, especially to the adoptee. Sometimes adoptive parents have a difficult time accepting and understanding the meaning of biology for the adoptee. Respecting the importance of the birth family in the adoptee's life allows the adoptee to embrace all that he or she is.

"Our family is anything but traditional! It usually takes quite a while to go through how everyone came into our family. But it

*is worth the time, because each person has a very personal story
that deserves explanation and attention. Needless to say, we are
quite open about adoption in our family!"*   *Adoptive parent*

In biological families, there are no questions about where
people come from or who is related to whom. It is
understood that everyone is related by blood and that
kinship ties exist among family members. Families of
adoption need to spend more time explaining the
relationship connections and dealing with the feelings that
arise because of the extended stories that are part of
adoption.

Handling Questions about Birth Parents

*"Once when my son was five, I was waiting at the school bus
with him. He turned to me and said, 'She must have been nice.'
I asked, 'Who?' He looked at me as if I were the dumbest
person living and said, 'The lady who 'borned me.' I asked him
why and he said, 'Because she gave me to you.' It melted my
heart right on the spot!"*   *Adoptive parent*

Adoptive parents sometimes fear questions about birth
parents. Not all questions about birth parents will be
difficult. Adoptive parents may even be surprised by their
child's insight and understanding of adoption issues.

*"I was always apprehensive about asking my adoptive parents
questions about my birth parents because they would get hurt
and upset. But I didn't know where else to go to get the
information."*   *Adoptee*

Talking about birth parents can be difficult for the adoptee
also. Adoptees turn to adoptive parents to obtain
information about their birth parents because they are a key
source of information. The adoptive parents are the link to

the birth parents since both were involved in setting up the adoption.

Adoptive Parent Perspective

"I think so rarely about my son being adopted that I have to remind myself that he is adopted. When I hear adoptees referred to as 'someone else's child,' I laugh. They don't have a clue."   *Adoptive parent*

"When my son was in the hospital, people would ask me if I was sorry that I had adopted him because he was having so many medical problems. I still can't believe it! My son is my son. I have never regretted adopting him. I love him more than the world."   *Adoptive parent*

Adoptive parents are parents. Adoptive parents consider their children to be their children, not their adopted children. Most adoptive parents enter into adoption with the understanding and commitment to raise the child as their own forever. It is usually those outside the triad who don't understand the permanence of adoption.

Fears about Birth Parents

"I had no choice when I gave up my children, but I never would have demanded them back. I remarried when my daughter was eighteen months old, but I didn't have the heart to take her away from the only parents she had ever known."   *Birth parent*

"Sure it occurred to me that I could try to get my son back. But when I thought about it, I knew that the reason I had decided on adoption was because I didn't feel I could take care of a baby. It still hurts a lot that I don't have him and won't be able to watch him grow up."   *Birth parent*

Birth parents will have lots of feelings about the adoption. It is natural for a birth parent to think about what it would be like to raise their child. Most birth parents do not want to change an adoption plan once it is in place, and only a very small percentage of birth parents take action to reclaim their child. If all parties in adoption have counseling, and especially if the birth parent considers the option of keeping the child, then there is less chance that a birth parent will try to reclaim a child.

Expectations of Adoptive Parents

"I can't believe the hoops we had to go through for this adoption. There were papers to sign, the home study, the research into how to adopt, the attorney fees, and the emotional drain of two adoptions that didn't work out."   Adoptive parent

It is expected that adoptive parents have received the "seal of approval" by "passing" all the tests required of them for an adoption. Pre-adoptive parents must go through a home study, get an attorney or go through an adoption agency, and have the money and the perseverance to get through the adoption maze. It can feel unfair that other parents don't have to expend as much time, energy, and money to parent a child.

"When I met my daughter, I found out that her parents had divorced when she was seven years old. I was furious! How could the agency have lied to me? They told me that the adoptive parents would be better parents than I could be. They told me that I was allowing my daughter to be in a secure and stable home - something that my social worker told me I could not give. I'd love to tell my daughter's adoptive parents about my happy twenty-three year marriage!"   Birth parent

Adoptive parents are expected to be stable, secure, financially fit, and able to provide a healthy environment in which a child can grow and prosper. Birth parents especially have expectations of adoptive parents since they are told or believe that adoptive parents will be better parents than they could be.

Acknowledgment of Differences

"When we began the whole process of adoption, we didn't want to believe that we were any different from any other family. Over time it has become obvious that our family does have specific issues to deal with because we are an adoptive family."

Adoptive parent

Adoptive families who acknowledge and embrace their differences are more flexible and tend to have more open communication. Acknowledging adoption allows all family members to be honest and express feelings in a safe environment. Adoptive families who acknowledge the differences created by adoption fare better than adoptive families who deny the differences of adoption. Pretending to be something you are not consumes energy and is draining. Being different is not bad. It is just different. Honoring the special aspects of adoption makes for a more functional adoptive family.

Triggers

"What do you say when a stranger compliments you on getting your figure back so quickly after giving birth?" *Adoptive parent*

"Sometimes I just want to yell at people! They are so rude! I really don't want to have to explain to everyone why my kids don't look like each other! It isn't anybody's business!"

Adoptive parent

Many people, especially those who are not touched by adoption, are insensitive to the issues and feelings of adoption. It is common for a full range of feelings to be triggered by a thoughtless comment or question. However, not every question requires an answer or response.

Sometimes an insensitive question is an opportunity to educate people about the issues of adoption. It can also be a situation that allows adoptive parents to show adopted children how to answer difficult questions.

9: Search and Reunion

"Just to see her would be a lifelong dream."   *Adoptee*

Who Searches?

"I really don't expect people to understand why I want to search. Who else but an adoptee or birth parent can really know the need I have to find my birth family?"   *Adoptee*

Searching involves adoptees and birth parents in closed adoptions. In open adoptions, there is no need for search because there is no secrecy about who the other triad members are. Search and reunion involve the adoptee and birth parent of the same triad finding each other and having a relationship.

Curiosity

"Isn't it natural to want to know where you come from? I can't believe how many people don't get that I just want to find someone who looks like me."   *Adoptee*

"I've never stopped wondering about what happened to my daughter. Is she OK? Does she know I think about her every day? I look at girls her age and wonder what she looks like. Does she have my hair color? Is she tall, like her birth father's family? How will I ever know unless I meet her someday?"
     Birth parent

"You could say that my curiosity was driving me crazy! I had to find her, to meet her, to know her, even if it was only for a moment. I tried to prepare myself for what my search probably had in store for me."   *Adoptee*

"I know how damaging it can be when you are not told the truth about your life when you are growing up. The feelings of emptiness, disconnectedness, not having a sense of real identity.

I always wanted to know my origins and roots. Now I have them after thirty-two years!"   *Adoptee*

Wanting to know your heritage and biological connections is natural. Most people know who their ancestors were and who their relatives are. In non-adoptive families, it is not considered odd to discuss who resembles who in the family and to comment on similarities. Only in adoption does the topic of origins become a twisted and secret subject.

Filling in the Blanks

"My daughter has had a good life. Her adoptive parents sound like they are exceptional people. They have given my daughter a life I could not have provided. I am glad to know this."

Birth parent

Birth parents in closed adoptions have questions about their children. Is the child OK? What was the adoptive family situation like? What does the child look like? Did their child get all that was promised? Is the child happy? Were the adoptive parents all that the social workers said they were?

"We are NOT looking for a 'Mommy,' contrary to what some people say. We had a mother. We just want to know who we are - a closing of the circle. We want to know 'Who am I?' and most often, 'Who do I look like?' and always, 'Why did you give me away?' But most importantly, we need our medical background."   *Adoptee*

Adoptees in closed adoptions also have many questions. Most of these questions can only be answered by birth parents. What non-adoptees know by simply looking at their relatives, many adoptees must seek.

"I have such an idealized vision of how my reunion with my birth mother will be. It is a fantasy that, I believe, has kept me going at times."   *Adoptee*

The hope of reunion and being able to fill in the blanks inspires many adoptees and birth parents to search for each other.

Medical Information

"When I began my search for my birth mother over ten years ago, I was hopeful that I would finally be able to have some semblance of a past family history. I was diagnosed with a rare heart condition that seemed to be passed on through my mother. I was also warned not to attempt to become pregnant and have children because I might not survive the process. Therefore, I needed medical information about her pregnancy and labor as well as her past and current physical health. It was upsetting and disappointing to find so many closed doors regarding my adoption. I stopped seriously searching about four years ago because I came up empty and lost faith that I would ever find out the truth of my existence."   *Adoptee*

Adoptees from closed adoptions do not know their medical history. If anything is known, it is usually about the health of the birth mother at the time of pregnancy and adoption, but much can change over the years.

"I got on the state registry because I had updated medical information for my daughter. My mother had recently died from colon cancer, which can run in families. I also found out that her birth father has colon cancer in his side of the family. The doctors told me she needed her medical history now! I contacted the adoption agency and told them if she ever contacted them to give her this medical information and my name if she ever wanted to contact me."   *Birth parent*

In closed adoptions, there is sometimes no way to let an adoptee and the adoptive family know about current medical information. A birth parent may leave information at an adoption agency for the adoptee, but may never know if the information has been passed on to the adoptee or the adoptive family.

"When people would ask me why I wanted to search for my birth parents, I would tell them that I had questions about my medical history. Most people can relate to wanting to know if cancer runs in your family. What people didn't know is that the medical information is not really the main issue. I wanted to know who I looked like and who my birth parents were and why they couldn't keep me."   Adoptee

Many adoptees will state that the reason they want to find their birth family is to know their medical history. This is usually a safe and valid concern and acceptable to others. People tend to think that wanting to know one's medical history is a legitimate reason to have curiosity about one's birth family. Many times, however, the medical information reason for searching is the tip of the iceberg and a smokescreen for other, deeper feelings.

Fears
"The thought of what I might find in my search scares me. What if she is dead? Then I would never get to know her. What if she denies being my birth mother? I don't know how I could handle wanting to know her but her not wanting to know me. Would I be interfering in the life she has been living after she gave me up? And if so, what kind of problems would my existence create? I don't want to hurt anybody, but I still want to find her."   Adoptee

"My greatest fear is that she won't want to meet me. My second fear is that she will never forgive me for giving her up."
                    Birth parent

It is natural to have fears about the search. Fears can paralyze a person into not searching or stopping the search process. Acknowledging fears by expressing them and deciding which fears are based in reality can free up energy to move on in the search process.

Synchronicity

"There are so many coincidences in my daughter's life and my own. When I was searching for her, she started writing me letters and keeping them in a box that she hoped she could give me some day. I had always kept a journal with my thoughts about her. The tears flowed when we exchanged our writing!"

Birth parent

Synchronicity refers to the seemingly coincidental occurrences between people and events. Many adoptees and birth parents describe synchronicity that occurred before or during their search. Synchronicity makes people feel connected to each other on a deep level.

Feeling the Connection

"When my daughter was seven, I began having uneasy feelings about her. My husband urged me to search, so I went back to the adoption agency to find out what I could. The social worker said their records showed that she was doing well in her adoptive family. Later, when I found my daughter, she told me that something was definitely wrong when she was seven - her parents were going through a divorce. She describes it as a very difficult time for her."

Birth parent

Many triad members describe feeling a connection to another triad member over time and distance. Perhaps it is the connection from the prenatal experience of pregnancy that continues on despite the separation. Perhaps it is a biological predisposition that makes our species continue on.

"Although she had chosen to put me up for adoption instead of keeping me, I still felt a bond to my birth mother. It was as if I had a void in my life, an empty space that could only be filled with her presence."   Adoptee

Searching can be driven by the strong connection between triad members. The desire to reconnect and to fill the empty space can persist no matter what else the triad member has in life.

"A sense of voice recognition was overwhelming. I'll never forget our very first phone contact. My birth mother's voice seemed so soothing, so.... mother like."   Adoptee

There are many different ways to feel the connection between birth parent and adoptee. Human beings use all their senses to identify people and situations. The more senses that are involved, the more connected people will feel with each other. When the connection is made, there can be a feeling of rightness and familiarity.

Internal Searching

"I don't know how other adoptees walk through their lives, but I walk through mine searching. There has never been a time when I did not search faces in the crowd for one that looked like mine. I can't go to an airport or a public place without unconsciously searching. Is it her, is it her? I learned that my birth mother had polio as a young woman and walks with a slight limp. Now, every time I see a limping woman, my heart races as I search her face. Is it familiar? Is she the right age? Is it her?"   Adoptee

"I have been afraid to do an actual search for my son. I don't want to interfere in his life. But I do find myself thinking about him a lot and wondering how he is. I look into the faces of boys his age and wonder about him."   Birth parent

Many adoptees and birth parents search for each other in a quiet, unspoken way. This internal search process involves looking in crowds for the person, wondering where the other person is, and wondering how the other person is doing. Some people are aware of the energy they are expending on this internal search process and some are unconscious of the extent of their mental activity.

External Searching

"I want to know and meet my birth parents. I hope that someday this will happen. I have the need to know who I am and what I am made of. A lot of times I feel very empty and alone. I do have my own family, but I still have a very large void in my life. This void can only be filled with my birth parents."   *Adoptee*

For many triad members, the internal search crosses over and becomes an external search. Wanting to know begins to outweigh the fears of searching. Many triad members who search are looking to fill the void they feel. This void is caused by not having full information.

"I am denied my medical information because of sealed records. This has always bothered my adoptive parents and now, as a parent myself, it really bothers me. I think that if I can just find my birth mother and ask her some questions, I will be able to peacefully get on with my life."   *Adoptee*

Many times the desire for medical information begins the external search. The closed doors and sealed records of closed adoption make it difficult to gain access to the information necessary to complete a search. There can be much frustration, disappointment, and anger at what people need to go through to have a successful search.

"I think that more than wanting to find my birth parents, I want to find myself. The search process has led me to many wonderful people and allowed me to know myself better. I suppose you could say that I am making the most out of a difficult situation!"   Adoptee

"I feel like I need to tell him why I gave him up. I don't want him to go through life thinking I didn't love him or want to raise him. I want the reassurance that his life was better than what I could have given him."   Birth parent

External searching is a very personal process that allows the searcher to gain more awareness of him- or herself and of the issues involved. For many people, searching is a way to complete the picture and to rest easier about previous decisions.

Deciding to Search

"I really struggled with whether to tell my adoptive parents that I wanted to search for my birth parents. I wasn't sure if they would be supportive or not. I talked to a lot of people in my triad support group about it and finally decided to tell my parents. At first they were hurt, but then we were able to talk about all of our feelings and they understood my need to search. I'm glad I did tell them because it helped us to talk more about adoption and they had information that helped me to find my birth mother."   Adoptee

"I didn't tell my parents about my decision to search for my daughter because they were so unsupportive when I was pregnant with her. I did tell my sister though, and she was really there for me. It brought us closer because in a way it healed our relationship too."   Birth parent

Deciding to search can be a real turning point for adoptees and birth parents. The decision is usually made after much consideration and marks the beginning of an unknown journey. Deciding to search can also be a time to open up about adoption feelings and issues. Along with deciding to search, adoptees and birth parents must also decide who they are going to tell about their decision to search. It is natural for old wounds and current fears to arise when making the decision to search.

"After my adoptive parents had died and my children were reaching the age of starting their own families, I felt the need to see what I would be able to find out. If nothing else, I wanted some health history to pass along to my children and grandchildren."   Adoptee

It is not unusual for adoptees to decide to search after their adoptive parents die. Adoptees worry about how their adoptive parents will react to the decision to search and try to avoid conversations about searching. One disadvantage of waiting until adoptive parents die is that they sometimes have information that will help in a search. Also, by that time, birth family members may also have died.

"When I finally got around to seriously searching for my birth mother, I found out that she had died six years earlier. Then I tried to find my birth father. He had been dead for ten years. I sometimes wonder what it would have been like to have searched earlier and found them when they were alive. It leaves unanswered questions. But I'm still glad I did do the search. At least I know now."   Adoptee

Deciding to search can come at any time. Most who decide to search do not regret their decision, no matter what they find out. Knowing that time is limited can inspire one who is hesitant to search.

Obsessiveness of Searching

"I'm searching, dreaming, longing for answers. I think of nothing else. I have an unrelenting desperation to find you. During work I look into the eyes of my customers and wonder if those are your eyes. I look for signs while asking myself, 'Do I look like this person?' I fantasize many things while I search for you. I'm told this is normal!"   *Adoptee - journal entry*

Whether it is the internal searching or the external searching, there can be a constant craving for information about the person being sought. Continually thinking about someone is a way to keep them alive in one's heart and mind.

"My life became consumed by searching for my son. I was always waiting for a phone call, or a letter, or going to a support group meeting. I couldn't think of anything else."

Birth parent

Searching can become a full-time job for triad members. Many who search seem obsessed and driven in their pursuit of finding people and information. The activities of searching, writing letters, making phone calls, and going to meetings, are a way to manage the feelings that surface during a search.

Adoptive Parents and the Search

"I wanted to find my birth mother for most of my life. My mother told me that once I graduated high school and felt I was ready, she would do everything she could to help me find my birth mother. My mother told me that she wanted to meet my birth mother someday so she could thank her."   *Adoptee*

Some adoptive parents are very supportive of their child's desire and interest in searching for birth parents. These parents are usually open with any information they may have about the birth family and are aware of the importance of the birth family to their child

"My life has been good. I always knew I was adopted and was told that I was chosen. My adoptive mother tries to support my search, but she is scared. Scared that I will never find my birth mother and that I'll be disappointed. Scared that I will find my birth mother and be rejected. But most of all, I think she is scared that if I do find my birth mother, and make a connection, then her place will be jeopardized. In her head she knows that is not so, but in her heart is another story!" Adoptee

Adoptees are very aware of the feelings their adoptive parents may have about the search. Some adoptees do not tell their adoptive parents about searching for fear of hurting their feelings or of having to defend their need to search. Other adoptees will talk about the search but will hold back some of their excitement, not wanting to upset the adoptive parents.

"I am definitely supportive of my son searching for his birth mother, and we have given him all the information we have to help him. Sometimes I get very teary and sad about the thought of losing him to someone who he may feel more connected to. I try not to show him the sad feelings because I want him to do what he needs to do." Adoptive parent

Even very supportive adoptive parents can have mixed feelings about the search. Searching can take adoptive parents back to the time of adopting and raise earlier fears and feelings. It is important to acknowledge and validate all feelings that come up around search for all the triad members.

"Because of the extreme differences with my adoptive family, I have always had a strong desire to find my birth mother although guilt and loyalty have stopped me from searching time

and time again. I would encourage all adoptive parents to put their own egos aside and help their adopted children search and learn about their natural family. Not to do so can keep a child in denial, or worse, in resentment and fear."   Adoptee

Adoptees tend to have a strong loyalty to their adoptive parents. It is important for adoptive parents to realize that searching is not a statement about adoptive parenting. Searching is a personal need to find out information about oneself.

"At age thirty, after giving birth to two daughters, I decided to search for my roots. My adoptive parents nearly disowned me, and they never felt the same towards me. It turned everything upside down. But it was worth it."   Adoptee

Searching can feel very threatening to adoptive parents. Some adoptive families do not handle adoption or search issues very well. Searching is not an insult to the adoptive family. Searching is an attempt to know one's history and fill in the missing pieces.

Wanting to Find the Truth

"I am currently searching for my birth family. My physician has recommended that I try to contact them because I know absolutely nothing about my medical background. Personally, I wish to have a life synopsis of my birth family so that I may know my ancestors' struggles and triumphs."   Adoptee

"I don't want to intrude on his life or take over from his adoptive parents. I just want to know that he is all right and that his life is working out for him."   Birth parent

Triad members have various reasons for wanting to search. Adoptees want to know their history. Birth parents want to know how their children are. The basic underlying reason for searching is wanting to know the truth.

The Right to Know

"Not having the right to know your parents seems illegal."

Adoptee

"I only want the answers that are rightfully mine. I do not wish to cause anyone trouble or pain. I don't even expect to be loved. I just want to have the answers to the past and to my beginnings. I will accept whatever those answers are. And then I shall be at peace."

Adoptee

Adoptees come to the decision to search by realizing that they have a right to know who they are, where they come from, and who they are related to. Believing in one's right to know adds strength to the desire and footwork necessary in the search process.

"Many people have told me that I don't have a right to search for my son. They say that I signed the papers twenty-five years ago and that I can't go back on my word now. I agree with them to some extent. But how can I ever rest if I don't know if he is OK? I have some rights as a mother."

Birth parent

Many birth parents struggle with the decision to search. At the time of relinquishment, they made a decision and signed an agreement to release their child. However, they seldom foresaw the emotional impact of their decision.

"My opinion of the adoption triangle is - the adoptee was an innocent part of it and should legally be allowed to have all information when reaching legal age. The birth parents should not expect one hundred percent privacy when the adoptee reaches adulthood. The adoptee has a right to search for them. The adoptive parents should prepare for this also."

Adoptee

The right to search is an emotionally laden issue. Anyone contemplating adoption today must be aware of what the triad members of the past can share. In a closed adoption, triad members will wonder about each other. Some triad members will want to search and will try to locate family members. If search is too threatening an issue for potential adoptive parents or potential birth parents, then options other than adoption need to be considered.

Treatment of Those in Search

"I have searched for twenty-eight years now. I have been told that adopted children (I was forty-two at the time) have no right to their information. I was asked how I could be so ungrateful to my adoptive parents by searching. I was asked why I wanted to search since my birth mother didn't want me and gave me away."   Adoptee

"My husband really doesn't understand my need to find my son. He thinks I should let it alone. I think he feels threatened by my intense interest in locating my first born child. My parents have also backed away and think I'm foolish to search. Thank God I have my support group that understands and supports my search."   Birth parent

"Why would my daughter want to find her birth mother? If her birth mother wanted her in the beginning, then she would have kept her."   Adoptive parent

Searching is, in and of itself, emotionally difficult and overwhelming. No one decides to search impulsively. Much thought goes into deciding to search. Added to this are the responses of those around the triad member. Many who decide to search are treated badly and with disrespect, or are questioned about their motives and told to leave the past in the past. Sometimes their only support comes from other triad members who believe in the right to search.

Where to Start

"I am very interested in finding my birth father. One way I thought of trying to find him was to go to Minnesota and drive

around on the buses.   He was a bus driver and so was his brother."   *Adoptee*

Where does one begin a search? It can be overwhelming to try to figure out how to go about starting a search. Sometimes there is very little information to go on besides a bit of a story here or there.

"I didn't know where to start when I began my search. Someone had suggested that I go back to the adoption agency and see if I could put a letter in the file for my daughter. I was surprised that they let me do that. It was easier than I thought it would be."   *Birth parent*

When beginning a search, it can be productive to go back to the beginning - the adoption agency or the attorney who handled the adoption. In some agencies, adoptees and birth parents can leave a letter for the other person in the file. Some agencies even facilitate reunions for adoptions that took place in their agency. Sometimes agencies can give information about where to go next.

"We didn't have very much information but we gave our daughter all that we had. I wish we had more, it is painful to see how difficult it is for her to run into dead ends all the time."   *Adoptive parent*

Another way to start a search is by asking adoptive parents for all the information they have about the birth family. Sometimes information can be found in the story of how the adoption took place or who the professionals were in the adoption. In a legal adoption, there is always some kind of paperwork involved with original information such as a name, city, or even a Social Security number. Clues will surface through various means.

Reunion Registries

"I was sent information about search groups and a form to fill out for the state reunion registry. I filled out the form and sent it back to be filed. I was told that if my birth mother had also registered, both of us would be contacted regarding the match and we would decide if we wanted to meet. I never got a phone call from them. I found out later that my birth mother didn't know about the registry, so she never filled out a form." Adoptee

Reunion registries can be very effective if people know about them and how they work. To register, the adoptee and the birth parent send in information about themselves and what they know about each other. This information is matched with other information received by the registry. If a match is made, each party is notified. Reunion registries do not necessarily cross-connect with each other. So, if an adoptee registers with one search group registry and the birth parent registers with another, there may not be a match even though each person has registered.

"I had the Soundex form for a few weeks before I sent it in. I really wanted a reunion but figured it would happen in the distant future. I guess filling out the form made me realize that a reunion was really possible. I had to think about whether I was ready and what I would find."   Adoptee

Many organizations and states have their own registries. It is best to register with as many registries as possible to cover all the bases. The International Soundex Reunion Registry is an international registry that is free of charge.

"I've always wondered what happened to the other girls who were in the maternity home with me. It felt as if we got so close when we were there - even though they didn't want us to. Since we were only allowed to use our first names there, I wouldn't know how to contact anyone. Sometimes it feels as if it would be

nice to talk with someone else who was there - my memory gets
pretty clouded when I think back to that time."   Birth parent

There are other registries that may be helpful. The National
Maternity Home Registry allows women to make contact
with other women from the same maternity home. Making
the effort to register on any registry can be an empowering
and healing step.

Search and Support Groups

"All of us adoptees deserve to have answers. We pray, we hope,
we wonder, we hurt, and we love. We also share that empty hole
inside, the gap in our soul. We are like family, holding on until
our search is over, giving each other strength to go on."

Adoptee

Support is very important before, during, and after a search.
It can be very comforting to be with a group of people who
understand the feelings and issues that one is experiencing.

"No one else understood my desire to search. Friends would
say that I should leave well enough alone and not look for him.
But the people in my support group did understand and did
support my search. I don't know what I would have done for
support without the group."   Birth parent

Many people outside the triad have difficulty understanding
the desire and emotional need to search. Being in a search
and support group validates feelings and helps people move
forward with their search.

"I didn't really understand my daughter's need to search before
I attended the triad support group meetings. When I heard the
other adoptees talk about searching and saw the tears they shed,
I was able to be more supportive of my daughter searching for
her birth mother."   Adoptive parent

Many support groups are open to all triad members. Participating in a support group allows one to better understand one's own feelings and those of other triad members.

Continuing to Search

"And so my search continues - on and off for nearly twenty years. My progress is slow. I have run into countless brick walls. I'm beginning to lose hope, to think that I will never find her. Maybe she doesn't even exist. What's the point anyway? But then I continue for fear of time running out. I fear that it will be too late."   *Adoptee*

Searching is not an easy task, but sometimes not searching is even harder. Closed records lock many doors. It can take great determination to continue to look for the one door that may contain the valuable information one is seeking.

Internal Timing

"I had searched on and off for fifteen years, never getting anywhere and letting other things in my life take priority. Then one day I just knew it was time to get serious about finding my birth mother. I asked around and hired a searcher, knowing I probably would not be able to complete a search on my own. I was willing to risk finding out whatever there was to find."

Adoptee

Taking up the search involves an internal shift where the desire to know outweighs the complacency of not knowing. Action may begin by writing letters, joining a support group, or hiring a searcher. Knowing the truth becomes more important and pressing than keeping the secret.

"One day I just got really mad. How dare people say that I can't know my medical history, or my origins, or my birth

family! I decided that no one was going to stop my search. I had heard all the reasons about why I shouldn't search - it would be intruding, I was rocking the boat, I was hurting my adoptive parents. But those reasons don't matter anymore. I now know that it's OK for me to search."   Adoptee

"I'm fifty-four years old. It's about time I stopped listening to my mother and searched for my son."   Birth parent

Sometimes anger motivates an adoptee or birth parent to search. They have kept their feelings inside for a long time and finally feel entitled to search. For some people, searching is the first time they have stood up for themselves or acted assertively. The search then becomes a statement of acting on one's own behalf.

Knowing versus Not Knowing

"Discovering the truth is better than remaining in limbo with haunting, unanswered questions and unresolved feelings."

Birth parent

For most people who search, knowing is better than not knowing. No matter what they find out, they find fulfillment in knowing the truth rather than continuing to wonder.

"Now I can truly move on in my life. I know who I am and who I am related to. Before I found my birth family, I had to guess at my history. People would say things that upset me because I didn't have the answers to where I came from. Now things are smoother and easier."   Adoptee

The shift from not knowing to knowing can be dramatic and can affect many parts of a person's life. The sense of being able to integrate the whole picture of who one is allows the people to move on in their life.

The Power of Searching

"It took a lot to get to the point of beginning my search. Looking back, I see that I gained a lot by searching besides finding my birth mother. I met people in a support group who have become close friends. I'm not afraid to state my opinions about adoption anymore. I feel as if I have accomplished the impossible and lived to tell about it!"   Adoptee

There is more to the search than just searching. People learn how to be resourceful and continue on when things don't look promising. Many also learn how to ask for help and get support. The process of searching can teach people many lessons about life and relationships.

"I found my son six months ago, and he has chosen not to meet me. This would have devastated me had I not been in a search and support group while I was searching. During my search, I had prepared myself for any outcome. The friendships I have made from the group have gotten me through this rough time. While I was searching, I learned a lot about myself and my abilities. My search was not in vain at all - I found my best qualities."   Birth parent

The power of searching is seen in the strength people gain during the process. Much growth and healing can take place while searching, for it offers an opportunity to open up to others, to get support from others, and to become aware of one's own hidden qualities.

Waiting to be Found

"I haven't searched yet. I'm hoping that my birth mother will call me. I worry about disrupting her life and whether anyone knows about me. I suppose that if I don't hear from her in a few years then I may start looking for her."   Adoptee

"I don't know if it would be fair to knock on my daughter's door. What if she was never told that she was adopted? What if

she doesn't want to meet me? I will let the choice be hers
whether to contact me or not."   Birth parent

Some people are waiting to be found. Rather than taking up
the search themselves, those who wait hope that the other
person will find them. It can feel safer to wait to be found.
Searching is a process that requires courage, persistence,
and the willingness to face the risk of rejection.

"I would love it if my birth mother found me. It would mean that
she really cared about me."   Adoptee

Many people who sit and wait for the other person to find
them have the fantasy that they will be found. To those
who wait and want to be found, being found represents love
and concern.

Not Wanting to be Found

"I have called my birth mother two or three times and wrote a
lot to try to convince her to just talk with me. She has never
written back except one time to tell me to keep on being me and
that she never nurtured or raised me to be who I was, and that
was that. Years have gone by, and I only called her one other
time and thought she was caving in and accepting the fact that I
just wanted to talk or to meet as we are both adults now. We
never met or talked, and I don't bother to write or call anymore,
but I still look in the phone book just to make sure she is still
there and still alive."   Adoptee

Not everyone wants to be found. Some people are not
ready to be found or feel it is best to not have any
connection with the past. It can be painful for the person
who searched to find someone who doesn't want contact,
and the searcher may need time to integrate another
experience that feels like loss and rejection.

"I found my birth mother in 1980, and she was not happy to see me. I also found a half-sister and grandparents. Through the years, my birth mother and I have called, visited, and written. But no real closeness. It used to bother me, but I have accepted it now. The void in me is smaller due to me finding some of my relatives, getting information from them and photos. I feel more complete and at peace."   Adoptee

Sometimes other relatives found in a search are interested in maintaining a relationship. Having some connection with some relative generally feels better than no contact at all. No one can take the place of the person being sought, but other relationships can ease the disappointment and provide information.

Initial Rejection > Agreement to Meet

"When my daughter first contacted me, I was in shock. How did she find me? What did she know about me? Had she told anyone in my family about her existence? So many questions were running through my head. All I could say to her was that I wasn't able to meet with her. It took me close to a year to feel comfortable enough to set up our first face-to-face meeting."

                                                    Birth parent

"I didn't know what to do when my birth mother first contacted me. My parents were sitting there in the room when I got the letter, and I felt really uncomfortable. I was sixteen at the time. I wrote her back and told her that I was happy and that I didn't want to meet her. Later, when I was twenty, I contacted her again and told her I was ready to meet her. I guess it was just too much at the time when I was younger."   Adoptee

Sometimes people just need time to adjust to the initial shock of being found. With time and patience, an initial "no" can turn into a "yes." It is important to respect the other's responses, whatever they are, and to understand that they have their own personal reasons for their reactions.

Intrusion

"I have always been hesitant to contact my birth family because I know that I embarrassed them. I do not know my birth mother's or birth father's marital status at the time of my adoption."   Adoptee

"I am torn between my need to search for my daughter and my desire to respect her privacy. Will she think that I am intruding into her life?"   Birth parent

People who search know that searching and finding will have consequences. Some searchers worry that contacting the other person will be seen as an intrusion. Adoptees are usually aware that their birth may still be a secret in their birth parents' lives. Birth parents typically know that their child may be surprised by contact.

"I always felt something was missing - now I'm trying to fill that hole with my search. But do my biological parents want to be found?"   Adoptee

Searching means walking into unknown territory. Searchers can't know how someone is going to react to being found until they find them.

Intuition

"I was aware of using my intuition when I was doing my search. When I had decisions to make about which way to go, I would just make the choice that felt right at the time. My gut never steered me wrong!"   Adoptee

"I feel as if I had shut off my maternal feelings the day I left the hospital after giving birth to my daughter. I wonder if it will come back when I find her."   Birth parent

Searching can be a time when people reconnect to their intuitive self. We are all born with a sense of intuition, a variety of senses, and a knowing that guides us throughout our lives. For many in the adoption triad, intuition has gone underground to make way for socially acceptable thoughts and feelings about adoption.

Empowerment

"I never truly realized what emotions I had until I began my search. I had, as well, strength I was not aware of."   Adoptee

Searching can be a time of true empowerment. Searching brings up feelings and emotions that must be addressed. Strength comes from facing these emotions, dealing with them, and realizing that not everyone has the courage to struggle with such raw feelings.

"I didn't have a choice about being adopted but I did have a choice about deciding to search for my birth family. What I found was much, much more."   Adoptee

"Choosing to look for my son was a difficult decision. I struggled with it for so long. I finally realized that to search for him would be taking a stand and letting him know that I had some regrets with the choice I had made when he was born."
Birth parent

Control is an issue for all triad members. Choosing to search is a way to feel in control. For many, the process of searching and the choices made along the way are empowering.

Death at the End of a Search

"Finding death at the end of my search is a tragedy that will forever burn in my heart with great anguish, but I have never been sorry that I did my search. As I continue to piece together the fragments of my life, I know I would have never felt complete without my search."   Birth parent, son deceased

For those who find death at the end of their search, the search is not in vain. There is a peace that comes at the end of any search, no matter what the outcome. Searching is always a journey of personal gains and possible losses.

"By the time I completed my searches, both my birth mother and birth father were deceased. But we did track down my birth mother's sister who was very surprised and happy to hear from me. She was the oldest in the family and could remember when my birth mother had me at fifteen years old. I went to visit her and enjoyed the pictures and family stories."   *Adoptee*

If the person being looked for has died, other relatives may be available who can fill in the missing pieces of the puzzle. Strong and healing relationships can be made with these relatives.

Is It Worth It?
"I hope that everyone who has been adopted will find a way to find out who their birth parents are. This took me almost eight years, and both my birth parents were deceased, but it was well worth the effort."   *Adoptee*

"Would I do it all over again? Absolutely! Searching took every ounce of energy I had, but now I can sleep at night."
                                        Birth parent

It is impossible to put a price on one's emotional well-being. Searching takes time, emotional energy, and sometimes money. It forces a person to be patient and tolerant. It provides opportunity to vent anger and to open one's heart to others. As with all of life's challenges, search can teach valuable lessons not possible in any other circumstances.

10: Reunion Relationships

"What a roller coaster this reunion has been!"   *Birth parent*

Continuation of a Previous Relationship
"I knew him but I didn't. I was looking for my baby and found a grown man! He is a mix of my family, his birth father, and his own personality. It has been a joy getting to know him!"
                                                    Birth parent

A reunion is the continuation of a previous relationship. Intimate strangers come together again with few memories and a deep bond.

"Our telephone reunion lasted over four hours. Our conversation was filled with talk of our personalities, families and personal histories. I also found out about my birth father."
                                                    Adoptee

The first contact between birth parent and child is usually by letter or by phone. It is not unusual for initial reunion conversations to cover many topics and last for hours. Catching up after years of separation is no small task!

Impact of Initial Contact
"During the time after the initial contact with my birth mother and just prior to my returning her call, I cried on and off with tears of joy and for the feeling of wholeness that began to seep into my pores. My emotions were very intense. I was on cloud nine. Was this really happening to me? Yes, it was."   *Adoptee*

It can be hard to believe that the reunion has actually happened. Many emotions can rush to the surface. Some will be expected, some will be surprising.

"I couldn't believe it when my daughter called. I had waited twenty-five years for this day. I carried the first letter she wrote to me and her picture everywhere I went! I would practically stop strangers to tell them that she had found me. I was in heaven!"   *Birth parent*

To many, reunion is a lifelong dream that can be intoxicating, exhilarating, and unbelievable. To those who want to be found, a reunion is to be savored, held, and cherished.

The Joy of Connecting

"I hope that every adopted child and birth mother in the world are able to enjoy the process of reunion if it is in their hearts."
Adoptee

It is almost impossible to describe the range of feelings that can occur when a mother and her child reunite. Perhaps it is similar to the connection that happens when a mother gives birth. Reuniting is like welcoming home a long lost, but never forgotten, friend.

"One of the first things I mentioned to my birth mother in our initial conversation was that I loved music. To this she responded, 'I knew it!' She explained that she was enrolled in the school of music at the university when she became pregnant. She then told me a story, that when she was nine months pregnant she went to a symphony concert. They were playing something very energetic by Beethoven, and I began to kick and move. "You knocked me out of my seat!" My birth mother had fully expected me to love music. I told her I did love music - especially the drum. I remember thinking - God, is this really happening? My life has been filled with the joy of this call every waking moment since. I have told and retold this story to many friends, bringing joy to all who I have shared this with."
Adoptee

There is nothing quite like the reunion experience. It is a dream come true and a time that becomes etched in one's mind. A reunion involves getting to know someone so familiar and yet unknown.

Honeymoon Period

"I remember when I first saw her and held her in my arms. It was like holding myself. I felt as if the missing part of my life had now gone full circle. We couldn't get enough of each other. We talked constantly and visited very often. She and I live only one-and-a-half hours from each other and have for twenty-six years. Our phone bills totaled almost $500 the first month! Now, after eighteen months, we have finally calmed down."

Birth parent

There is a kind of honeymoon period in reunion relationships that begins at the point of contact and lasts for some time. It can be similar to the falling-in-love period at the beginning of romantic relationships when everything seems magical and wonderful.

Expectations

"The reunion has exceeded all of my expectations! I couldn't have hoped for a better relationship."

Adoptee

"One thing I learned from my reunion experience is not to expect anything. Take it one day at a time. Expect to feel vulnerable."

Birth parent

Both parties need to explore their expectations about the reunion relationship before it happens. Expect anything and be prepared for everything. Many past and present emotions arise for those involved in a reunion relationship.

Fantasy Meets Reality

"I had fantasized about her for my entire life. It took some time for me to realize that she was who she was and not who I wanted her to be."   Adoptee

A lack of information can provide fertile ground for fantasy. Many reunions occur when the adoptee is an adult, allowing many years for a fantasy to be created.

"I never dreamed a reunion could be such a bittersweet affair. When you see reunions on television they are happy. No one tells you what happens after."   Birth parent

Those who enter a reunion relationship will bring with them their personal fantasies about the other person and about what the reunion relationship will be like. A reunion can go better than expected or leave much to be desired. It is important to allow the reality to replace the fantasy.

Regression

"Meeting my son made me feel sixteen again. I found myself giggling and acting so young. I had to keep telling myself to act my age! Plus, he looked so much like his birth father."
                                        Birth parent

It is not uncommon for people in reunion to regress back to the time of the relinquishment. The birth parent can again feel confused, young, and unsure of what to do. The adoptee can feel like a helpless infant. Both parties can feel as if they have lost touch with their adult self.

"I kept wanting her to mother me in some kind of way but I just wasn't sure how."   Adoptee

The reunion will bring up issues of parenting and needs. Regression can make it difficult to distinguish between current needs and past needs that didn't get met.

Adjusting

"All of a sudden I have gone from being an only child to having five brothers and sisters and tons of aunts and uncles. I love it, but it is also a lot to handle and get used to." Adoptee

There is a lot of adjusting that needs to take place in reunion relationships. People go in search of one person but can be surprised to find that many other people are also involved. It can take some time to integrate new relatives into one's life.

"My son reminded me that his son's birthday is coming up. I'm not surprised that my son has a son, but it's taken me a while to own the identity of being a grandmother!" Birth parent

Sometimes people require time to adjust to who they are and to the roles they occupy. A birth mother may feel ready to be a mother to her son, but she may need more time to incorporate the role of being a grandmother too.

Searching versus Being Found

"When I got the call from my daughter, I didn't know what to say. I was totally unprepared and probably sounded a little off-putting. After I took her phone number and got off the phone, I felt a wave of emotions wash over me. I cried on and off for a few days and didn't really know why." Birth parent

Typically, the person who searches is more ready for a reunion than the person who is found. Searchers have had time to think about their actions and feel their emotions, whereas the person being found may need time to catch up in their thoughts and feelings.

Going Away Again

"Unfortunately, my daughter has backed off considerably since our reunion. I'm trying to understand and give her time and space, but the truth is I don't understand. She was so happy and excited in the beginning. Now she has hardly anything at all to do with me. I feel as if I have to let go of her all over again."

Birth parent

There are ebbs and tides in reunion relationships. Respecting the other person while dealing with one's own feelings is no small task. Many people in reunion relationships fear that the other person will leave. If the reunion relationship falters or ends, it feels as if the other person has gone away again.

Walking on Eggshells

"I get a sense when talking with my birth mother that she is very sensitive to what I say. I feel as if I need to be a little cautious around her and not hurt her feelings."   *Adoptee*

"So often I feel as if I need to watch what I say to my daughter. I'll listen for changes in her voice and wonder if I have said something that has upset her. I feel as if I have to walk on eggshells around her."   *Birth parent*

Many people in reunion describe a sense of unsureness in the relationship. They feel they must walk on eggshells to preserve the fragile bond. Some worry about whether they will say the right thing or hurt the other person's feelings.

Communication Skills

"I am such an adult in other relationships, but when I talk with my birth mother I lose that sense of being direct. Sometimes I feel like I'm not making sense at all."   *Adoptee*

"I wasn't sure what to write to my son after we had our first conversation on the phone. I had lots of stories, but I didn't

know how much he wanted to know. I wasn't sure how involved he wanted to be. It was sort of like the ultimate blind date - one wants to give a good impression but try not to be impressive."

Birth parent

Some people who enter a reunion relationship already know effective communication skills. Some people are so overcome by the emotions of a reunion that they forget any communication skills they know. A reunion relationship can offer people an opportunity to learn and apply important communication skills that can be used in all relationships.

"For four years, I never confronted my son or said anything that I thought would upset him. I swallowed all my feelings. Then my therapist suggested that I tell him about how I was feeling and state it in a way that made me own my feelings and not blame him. We practiced how I could say things, and it helped a lot. Now I feel like I can really talk to him and not hold back like I did before."

Birth parent

Using "I" statements is a basic and effective form of communication. Saying, "I feel _____ when you do _____" is direct and explanatory. Using "I" statements means being responsible for your own feelings and expressing them. Using "you" statements makes people feel blamed and defensive, which will create tension and misunderstandings.

"Sometimes I don't know what to do when my birth mother starts crying about things that happened in the past like when I was adopted. I can't really make it better for her, but I feel as if I should somehow."

Adoptee

Acknowledging the other person's feelings without trying to stop their feelings or fix them is another communication skill that is necessary in reunion relationships. No one can take away another person's pain. However, we can let a person know that we are sorry they feel the way that they do and ask if there is anything we can do to help.

Checking In

"I have learned to ask my daughter specific questions about our relationship and about how she is feeling. She has a difficult time expressing herself and doesn't always know how she feels. She says she likes me to be direct with her and that she's learning how to be more direct with me."   *Birth parent*

Checking in with the other person in a reunion relationship is crucial. Many fears and anxieties can be relieved by dealing with them directly.

"For a long time, I had this oppressive and obligatory feeling about communicating with my birth mother. I felt as if I was letting her down if I didn't call her all the time. I guess she felt the tension too, because one day she asked me what I thought of our relationship and was there anything we needed to discuss. I got brave and told her what I was feeling. We were able to work out a calling schedule that felt better for both of us. I'm really glad she brought up the topic."   *Adoptee*

Asking direct questions and giving honest responses allows a relationship to grow and prosper. Usually both people in a relationship can feel if there is tension. The fair and loving thing to do is to ask the other person how they are feeling about the relationship and to tell them how you are feeling.

Navigating the Relationship

"I didn't expect it to be perfect, but I guess I thought it would be less of a roller coaster!"   *Adoptee*

Navigating the reunion relationship takes time, patience and practice. There are ups and downs, times of feeling close and distant, and moments of clarity and misunderstanding. The relationship will have a life of its own and will need nurturing.

"This reunion relationship is probably the most difficult one in my life. I don't regret it, but I didn't realize how much energy it would take." Birth parent

Reunion relationships can be stormy, calm, and everything in between. The bond between parent and child creates a base on which to build a lasting relationship. Sometimes this bond feels tenuous and held together by a thread, while other times it can feel indestructible. Reunion relationships take energy and a commitment to work through the rough times.

Post-Reunion Feelings

"My life has totally changed. I don't look for my daughter's face every time I'm in a mall, on vacation, or in the grocery store. I am calm and not as depressed as I used to be. I still have some depression but nothing like before. I look at the pictures of my children and now they are all there. I guess you could say I'm complete." Birth parent

"I didn't want to meet her. I thought I would continue in my life and not have to tell anyone about her." Birth parent

Reunions bring up the past and force people to confront their current feelings. Adoption is not an easy experience. Reunion relationships can reflect the issues and feelings that have not been fully processed.

"I can move on now. I have the answers to the questions that I have wondered about my whole life. I don't have to wonder and wander anymore." Adoptee

Things change after a reunion. Many people feel a sense of serenity in knowing the truth and having information that wasn't available before. Many in reunion feel that they can now attend to other things in their life.

Impact on the Adoptive Family

"It took us a while to feel comfortable with our daughter finding her birth mother. We thought it meant that she hadn't gotten enough from us as parents. Over time we have talked about it, and now we know that she needed to understand herself more. We plan on meeting her birth mother sometime soon. I think we'll all be a little nervous at first."   Adoptive parent

"My parents' reaction to my birth mother finding me was surprise followed by a pause, and later, joy. My father mentioned that he would like to meet my birth mother someday and thank her for blessing them with me."   Adoptee

Some adoptive parents are thrilled when their child makes contact with his or her birth parents, but others feel personally offended by their child's search. It would be virtually impossible for adoptive parents to have no feelings about their child having a reunion relationship. Some adoptive parents will choose to be a part of the reunion, while others will choose to stay at a distance.

"I still can't get over the fact that my daughter found her birth mother. We were told that we would never see her or have contact with her. I cry every time I think about it. I just can't talk about it with my daughter."   Adoptive parent

Search and reunion can feel threatening to adoptive parents. A reunion can bring up the adoptive parent's worst fear - that the adoptee will want to be with the birth parents instead of the adoptive parents. Adoptive parents can fear being replaced by someone who wasn't there to do all the work of raising the child.

"Her parents are the best! Her mother and I have become very close friends. We have had them at our home for dinner, and we have been to their home on several occasions. We are all working very hard to make this work for our daughter."

Birth parent

The time of search and reunion can also be an opportunity for the adoptive family to come together around a topic that is important to all family members. Embracing the inevitable - that an adoptee has two families - can lead to closer relationships for everyone.

Reunion Realities

"I can't say everything has been perfect because it hasn't. Reunion has made lots of feelings surface in both of us. Some good, some not so good. Reunion for me has been very healing, and I believe it has for my daughter too. But painful at times also."

Birth parent

A reunion does not change the reality that an adoption took place. Perhaps the most difficult aspect of a reunion is the realization that the past cannot be replaced with the present. The adoptee has still lost growing up in the birth family, and the birth parent has still lost seeing their son or daughter grow up.

"It's been four and a half years since I was reunited with my biological parent. We've never been able to establish a relationship despite efforts on both sides. However, I'm still glad that I went through the process."

Adoptee

A reunion relationship may not go as well as expected. Everyone going into a reunion has personal expectations about the outcome. It is important to remember that there will always be a relationship, even if there is no contact at the present time.

Beyond the Triad

"Sometimes I think my son gets along better with my husband than he does with me! I guess it's the male bonding thing! I'm glad they do enjoy time together."   Birth mother

Connecting with a person close to the birth parent or adoptee can sometimes feel safer and less intense. The importance of these secondary relationships should not be overlooked as they can add greatly to the success of the primary reunion relationship.

"My grandmother and I bonded instantly and had a wonderful relationship until she passed away on Valentine's Day at the age of ninety-eight years old."   Adoptee

One of the joys of reunion relationships is being able to meet and get to know many people in a variety of ways. Those beyond the triad have also been affected by the adoption and may want to have a relationship.

Closing the Reunion Relationship

"We met several times and twice in my counselor's office. She picked me apart like an encyclopedia, got what she wanted, and asked to close the door."   Birth parent

Some people do not want to continue a reunion relationship. For them, meeting the person and getting information is all they were looking for. This can be difficult if the other party in the reunion does want an ongoing relationship.

"I really tried to have a relationship with her. I kept making attempts to see her and to help her. I know part of it is her limited capacity in many areas. She told me not to call her again. I've closed the door but not locked it."   Adoptee

Some people are just not emotionally available for a reunion relationship. It can be painful to give up a lifelong dream of having the relationship you've always wanted. As in any relationship, one can only control one's own actions and behaviors. Emotionally releasing the other person and closing the relationship is an option some will need to consider.

11: Before Choosing Adoption

"Isn't it ironic that the adoptee is the only one involved who doesn't have a choice in the adoption!"   *Adoptee*

Adoption as an Option
"We have had two failed adoptions. We were devastated. The second birth mother told us that she decided to keep her baby because a week before the delivery a social worker told her how she could get state assistance. Apparently no one had discussed that with her before."   *Adoptive parent*

Adoption is one of a number of options available to people with an unplanned pregnancy and to those who want to add children to their family. The decision to adopt or to relinquish a child must be well thought out with all the possible options considered. How can someone be sure that they want to relinquish their child for adoption if they haven't considered what it would be like to raise that child? How can people decide if adoption is a realistic option for them if they haven't considered living without children?

Research the Possibilities
"We thought a lot about what it would take to be adoptive parents. We looked into the different types of adoption and talked with friends and relatives who had adopted. We even went to a panel discussion where an adoptee, a birth parent, and an adoptive parent gave their views and experiences about adoption. It was really helpful to hear from people who had been there."   *Adoptive parent*

Adoption lasts a lifetime. Those considering adoption must research and consider the possible short- and long-term effects of such a major decision. Children are not returnable. The decision to adopt a child or relinquish a child for adoption has far-reaching and lifelong consequences for all involved.

"If I had to do it all over again, I think I would talk to other women who had given their children up for adoption. It never occurred to me that I would have feelings about this for so long. I thought that it would be over after I signed the papers."

Birth parent

Research the adoption option thoroughly. Find adoptees, birth parents, and adoptive parents and ask them about their experiences. Before making a decision about adoption, talk with at least five people from each of the triad positions to get an overview of what it is really like to live adoption.

Becoming a Birth Parent

"I never really chose to be a birth parent in a conscious sense."

Birth parent

Becoming a birth parent begins at conception. Every woman who gives birth is a birth mother. Every man who produces a child is a birth father. Conceiving a child and becoming a birth parent is a serious responsibility and a lifelong commitment. Relinquishing a child for adoption does not erase the responsibility that a birth parent has to a child. The genetic, familial, cultural, and blood ties will always connect parent and child, no matter who raises that child.

Becoming an Adoptive Parent

"We had thought about being parents for such a long time. We had made plans about family vacations and holidays. Then, finally, we got Amanda."   *Adoptive parent*

Becoming an adoptive parent begins in the imagination. Imagining being a parent motivates people to take the action steps that are necessary to initiate and to complete an adoption. This process of imagining and visualizing a child helps prepare adoptive parents for parenthood.

"I like to think that God had a plan for us and that it included not having biological children so that we could have Steven and Joshua in our lives. We had always thought of ourselves as parents, in fact we even talked about it on our first date. Obviously we had to adjust our picture of our life together, but it still turned out well."   *Adoptive parent*

Sometimes future expectations start very early. Some people see themselves as mothers or fathers from an early age. Some people start to see themselves as parents when they meet someone they care deeply about. Whatever the beginning time frame, wanting to parent can be a strong desire that does not go away. Adoption offers a way to be a parent and fulfill that dream.

What to Expect

"We really had no idea what to expect. We were so excited when the social worker said she had a baby for us. It was our dream come true. The minute we saw Stephanie, we fell in love with her. It felt as if she was meant to be in our family. We knew we had enough love for her, but we didn't know about all the needs she would have. I wish I knew then what I know now. It would have been easier for all of us."   *Adoptive parent*

Many prospective adoptive parents are not aware of all that will happen after they take their child home. The anticipation of finally having a child and creating a family can sometimes overshadow the realities of adoptive family life.

"We need to educate people about the fact that a woman who gives birth will not ever forget having a baby that she gave up for adoption and that at age eighteen it is okay for her to start

looking for that child. We need to convince adoptive parents not to feel threatened when the child they adopted wants to go looking for the birth parents, because if they've done a good job in bringing them up, they have nothing to worry about."

Adoptee

Education is a crucial part of adoption. A woman who is considering adoption for her unborn child and a couple who wants to adopt need to be aware of the many issues in adoption. All triad members will have feelings about adoption that will appear at various times. Exploring expectations and learning about adoption can prevent future difficulties and misunderstandings.

Choosing Adoption

"If you think you cannot adequately take care of a child, please love them enough to place them with someone who can. I can't tell you how many of our birth mothers, who, at the age of sixteen, decide that they want to parent,later realize what a horrible mistake they have made. Often they say that their mothers (who were also teen mothers) will take care of the child."   *Adoptee and adoption case worker*

Adoption is a choice birth parents make for their child. Adoption is also a choice for people who want to be adoptive parents. Adoptees do not have a choice in adoption. As in all important choices, the choice of adoption needs to be made with as much clarity as possible. The parties should have realistic expectations and be able to evaluate their own abilities and capacities honestly.

Choosing Adoptive Parents

"I had determined several parameters for the parents of my child. They were to be married longer than seven years, as most marriages end before that. They were to be religious; my child was to grow up knowing God. They had to like animals; I have always felt that those who are compassionate to animals will

have a greater love for their child, and the experience of life and death of animals is important. I wanted them to send him to college if he chose to go and to accept his decision if he chose not to go. The mother had to stay at home with him for the first few years, as I felt this would create a stronger bond with the family. I wanted a letter sent to me every year on his birthday. I wanted him to be raised with the knowledge that he was adopted. I wanted to regain custody if they both passed away as I did not want someone I did not know to raise him."

Birth parent

Birth parents may have a particular picture in their mind about who will raise their child. Because adoption becomes a consideration when the birth parents decide they cannot raise their child, they may have certain expectations about the prospective adoptive family. It is assumed that adoptive parents will have more to offer a child than the birth parents.

Choosing Birth Parents

"We had heard so many stories about birth parents deciding to keep their child after adoptive parents had paid for all the expenses. We were afraid that a birth mother might not be honest with us about drug use and who the father was."

Adoptive parent

Adoption is a leap of faith for all parties involved. Both the prospective adoptive parents and the prospective birth parents will feel doubts and apprehension. Those wanting to adopt may be frightened by current media stories depicting negative pictures of adoption interactions. Getting to know the prospective birth parents and asking them about their hopes for their child helps to build trust. Prospective adoptive parents who feel uncomfortable with a potential birth parent must be willing to walk away from that adoption.

Pre-Adoption Communication

"At first, it seemed they met all my criteria - they were even Catholic! But then, I was told that the mother would not stay at home and the father would. They began putting restrictions on me. Finally they contacted my attorney and told him that if the medical bills were more than $3,500, I would have to pay. I totally lost my cool. At that point, I decided that they wanted a status symbol, not a child, for they had placed a price on his head. They were not parents; they were yuppies who wanted another toy. My answer was 'No.' I wanted a better life for my child, better than mine, better than what I could give him, and this was definitely NOT it!"   Birth parent

"It was really touch-and-go for a while there. We thought we had it all worked out with the birth mother, and the attorney was telling us that things were going well. Then, the birth mother started getting more distant. She wouldn't return calls. We thought she had changed her mind. We were all ready to give up and start again with someone else. Then, when we did talk with her, we found out that she had felt totally overwhelmed and needed some time away from it all."   Adoptive parent

Pre-adoption communication can make or break an adoption. An adoption in the planning stages will be filled with emotions on everyone's part. It is not unusual to feel uneasy at times about both the proceedings and the other parties involved. Adoption is a process in which people need each other to fulfill their goals. Trust may or may not be present. Accepting a child into one's family and releasing one's child to others will be emotional. Having a safe place to honestly express one's feelings and concerns about the adoption is crucial to the adoption moving along as smoothly as possible.

Post-Adoption Communication

"We fully expected to have Susan (the birth mother) involved in our son's life. We had agreed to letters and pictures every four

months for the first year. We have kept our end of the agreement, but Susan has only written us once. Maybe it is too difficult for her. I worry about what effect it will have on our son."   *Adoptive parent*

"Things changed from our first meeting in the attorney's office to now, three years after the adoption. I guess I really wanted to believe that these people cared about me too. After the baby was born, we drifted apart and I got the feeling that they didn't want me around as much anymore. I don't know if I can blame them, but it sure feels weird."   *Birth parent*

Feelings can change from pre-adoption times to post-adoption times. It is impossible to know beforehand how one is going to feel about the adoption. Sometimes contact will go according to pre-adoption plans. In other cases, the feelings that arise after the adoption can cause people to not follow through with pre-adoption agreements. Sometimes another meeting after the adoption allows everyone to reassess their communication, expectations and abilities.

Transitional Nature of Feelings

"Now I know that the decision to release my son for adoption was right. I was not a victim. I was not a pawn. I had power. The adoption process was actually the best that it could be. I made those decisions and they were right. Of all the things in my life, those decisions surrounding the adoption were right. There is some peace in that."   *Birth parent*

"We were so crushed when the birth mother changed her mind at the hospital. We were in shock, actually. We thought we had done all the right things in working with her before the birth. Now, looking back on it all and having adopted another child from another birth mother, we can see that perhaps it was for the best that it didn't work out the way we thought it would. We are really happy with our daughter and wouldn't trade her for the world!"   *Adoptive parent*

During the adoption process, it can sometimes be difficult to be sure of anything. Doubts, fears, and anxiety cause people to question themselves, others, and the whole process of adoption. Many feelings will arise for all parties. Feelings in and of themselves are transitory in nature. Feelings come and go, some remaining the same over the years, and some changing over time.

Why Do You Want to Adopt?

"We just wanted to be parents. We spent so many years hoping for a child and going through infertility treatments that were horrendous and exhausting."   Adoptive parent

People want to be parents for a variety of reasons. Some reasons are noble and altruistic; others are self-serving and personal. Most people who consider parenting have a combination of reasons for wanting to parent.

"I'm so tired of people telling me that I should be grateful to my adoptive parents for raising me. Do non-adoptees hear things like that? Of course I'm grateful to my parents, but when do I get to stop paying the price?"   Adoptee

In any family, there are expectations for the parents and for the children, but in adoptive families there can be an added expectation about what the adoptive parents have done for the adoptee. Even though most adoptees are grateful to their adoptive parents, it would be unwise to enter into an adoption expecting to receive thanks. Adoption is about mutual needs and dependence. Adoptive parents become parents because of the adoptee, and the adoptee is raised by people wanting to parent.

"I think family ultimately means the willingness to love unconditionally above all else. It is hard for social workers to assess this in their pre-adoption visits, but anybody planning on

adopting hopefully knows themselves well enough to know if they have the capacity to love unconditionally. If they don't, then they shouldn't consider parenting."   Adoptee

Probably most people considering adoption believe themselves to be capable of unconditionally loving a child. Unconditional love involves loving someone for who they are, not for what they do, supporting them emotionally, and respecting them for their ideas, beliefs, and feelings.

"In my own case, the foster/adoptive family was severely abusive. There needs to be more screening and education! Although there's been progress in this field, I think it's far from perfect."   Adoptee and social worker

It is sad but true that some people become parents who do not have the capacity to parent. In adoption, this can take on added insult and injury because adoptive parents have "passed" the home study test and are expected to be capable and reliable parents. Any person who is thinking about parenting must seriously examine his or her capacity to care for, nurture, and respect a child.

Who Do You Want to Adopt?

"We held fast to the kind of child we wanted to adopt. We talked about it a lot and honestly revealed to each other what our limits were in terms of how old a baby would be and knowing the baby's background."   Adoptive parent

"At first, we thought we would only want a baby who was the same race as we are. Then, as we explored the options, it became clearer that there were so many children who didn't have any place to go and really needed parents right away. We finally decided that we wanted to adopt a toddler from another country."   Adoptive parent

Some people go into adoption with a fixed notion of the child they want to adopt. For other people, their initial picture can change over time and with more information.

"I don't think that many people realize how 'damaged' a child who has been freed for adoption may be, particularly if they've been abused and neglected. I think that adoptive parents generally need more education in terms of caring for a child who has been traumatized."   *Adoptee and social worker*

However much people may want to be parents, they must fully understand who is being adopted. Children are affected by their previous interactions. A child who has been in many previous placements or who has been abused or neglected will bring memories of the past and emotional, behavioral and interactional patterns with them into their new home. Adoptive parents must be aware of a child's past and prepared to address the needs rooted in previous experiences.

International Adoptions

"I think that I probably did have a better life being adopted than if I had grown up in Korea. However the '60s were a strange and difficult time to be a 'mixed' family. We lived in an all-white neighborhood, and the Vietnam War was going on. I strongly identified with the Vietnamese people I saw on TV because they were the only people around who looked like me."

Adoptee from Korea adopted by Caucasians

Adopting a child from a foreign country means added responsibility for the adoptive parents. An international adoptee is losing birth family, country, culture, history, and familiarity.

"I do not think that my parents really understood the pressures of what it would be like to be culturally different. I think they should have acquainted themselves with my cultural background

*and encouraged me to retain and learn Korean or another Asian
language."*   *Adoptee*

Attending to an adoptee's cultural heritage involves more
than an occasional trip to the country of origin or reading a
book on the culture. Culture involves the history, language,
food, and beliefs of a people. Cultural traditions are built
into every day living along with formal events and
ceremonies.

*"My parents did almost nothing to keep us in touch with our
culture. We once went to Ports of Call where my parents bought
my sister and me pins that had male and female wooden figures
dressed in Korean native dress. Actually, instead of making me
feel proud of being Korean, I felt ashamed."*   *Adoptee*

Sometimes the attempts of adoptive parents to introduce or
expose their children to the child's country of origin can be
met with mixed reactions. Adoptive parents can try to ease
the added losses of intercountry adoptions by joining
adoptive family groups that allow children of different
cultures to learn about their country of origin's culture and
to participate with other mixed-heritage families.

*"I don't think my parents understood or still understand what
growing up looking 'different' was like for me. Many times my
adoptive mother would point out mixed couples on television
and say that the husband was ashamed of his wife (the minority).
I've had to learn to discredit her remarks pertaining to my
ethnicity."*   *Adoptee*

Adopting internationally involves understanding the impact
of prejudice. If adoptive parents are of a majority race, they
may never have been the targets of prejudice. It is also
crucial for adoptive parents to look honestly and completely
at any prejudices they may have about any people. An

adoptee will be especially sensitive to the messages an adoptive parent conveys about the adoptee's country of origin.

"I would really like to know more about why I was adopted. I was told that my mother died and that was why I was in an orphanage. My adoptive parents say they don't know anything more. It seems like it would be impossible to find any birth relatives."   Adoptee from international adoption

For some adoptive parents, the option of adopting outside the United States seems appealing because there is a smaller chance of contact with their child's birth family. Although this might seem advantageous to the adoptive parents, the child is the one who will suffer the loss of birth family, culture, history, and being with people who are like him or her. Just because a birth parent is unavailable does not mean that the adoptee won't think about his or her birth parents.

Transracial Adoptions

"Our intention was to give Damon a better life. We didn't see him as a black kid; we just saw him as our kid. We knew his birth mother and had her blessings in raising him since she couldn't. Only now, as an adult, can Damon tell us about some of the things that were troubling him as a kid." Adoptive parent

Can a white person ever really know what it is like to be a black person? Should white parents adopt a black child? Should black parents adopt a white child? Transracial adoption is an emotional and complex issue.

"I know my parents tried to understand what it was like for me to be a black kid in a white family, but how could they know? I don't think they thought about what it would be like for me on

*the street. At home it was OK, but on the street I had to fend for
myself."*   *Adoptee*

It is impossible to know the future. A decision that is
rooted in good intentions can lead to consequences different
from what anyone had imagined. Perhaps those who adopt
transracially are not prejudiced. However, it is important
for parents who adopt transracially to understand that the
larger society and the neighborhood they live in may not be
as open-minded as they are. What will the impact be on
their child?

*"What I want to know is, who will that black kid go to when he
needs to talk about white people being down on him? His white
parents? I don't think so!"*   *Adoptee*

White parents may be members of the very group from
which the black adoptee is feeling prejudice. It can be
difficult for a child in a transracial family to go to parents
who have not felt the same feelings or been treated as the
adoptee has.

*"I'm black but I'm not. It's been a trip to figure out my racial
identity. My adoptive parents are white. My birth mother was
white and my birth father was black. I grew up in a mostly white
neighborhood but tried to find some other kids to hang out with.
Sometimes it was hard to be seen with my parents because then
I'd have to explain everything."*   *Adoptee*

People who are considering transracial adoption need to ask
themselves some very serious questions. What are they
willing to do to offer a child a culturally and racially rich
upbringing? Do they live in a mixed neighborhood? What
role models of their child's ethnic background will be
available? What prejudices do the adoptive parents have?
What will it be like for a child in a transracial family?

Adoption and Religion

"It was really important to me that my child go to people who were of the same religion I was.   I guess it was my way of holding onto something of her."   Birth parent

Some adoptees are matched with adoptive families of the same religion by request. The familiarity and comfort of religion can ease some of the anxiety about the adoption process.

"I found out that my birth father was Jewish.   This really surprised me and delighted me.   I had always been drawn towards people who were Jewish, and many of them actually thought I was Jewish too.   I was raised essentially without religion, so I liked the all encompassing energy of what I saw in my Jewish friends' families."   Adoptee

Some adoptees are raised in families that may embrace a religion that is different from that of the birth family. Religion is not only about belief systems but also about a way of life. Some religions have a cultural richness that is woven into everyday life.

"My parents were Orthodox Jews, and, in accordance with Jewish law, had me converted to Judaism during infancy. I was sent to a Jewish day school for first through eighth grades. During my first few years in school, I was constantly teased because I did not look Jewish. The stereotype was that all Jews have dark hair and dark eyes and I had white blonde hair and blue eyes. So, it seems that from early on I knew I was different and felt I did not belong."   Adoptee

As with many issues in adoption, those outside the adoptive family may hold views that differ from those inside the family. Religion is an issue of potential importance in the adoptive family.

12: Adoption Awareness

"Having other people voice the same feelings made me feel less crazy. Growing up, I had to keep pretending that adoption was not an issue."   *Adoptee*

Acknowledgment of Adoption Issues

"Two years ago, I would have said that being adopted has not affected me. Now, after reading books on adoption and going to support groups, I see that adoption has been my core issue all along. I was just dealing with all the other issues that got in front of it."   *Adoptee*

"We thought that giving them love and a good home was enough. When our son started acting up, we had to take action, and along the way, someone asked us about the kids being adopted. It never occurred to us that there was any connection."   *Adoptive parent*

Acknowledging that adoption is an issue is the first step in the healing process for triad members. Some triad members go through much of their lives feeling that adoption is not an issue for them. Others report a vague sense of feeling unsettled but not really paying attention to it. On some level, adoption issues are present for all triad members and will emerge at one time or another.

Validation of Feelings

"I couldn't believe that there were so many other people who felt like I did! It was painful to hear everyone's stories, but reassuring to know that other adoptees felt the same way I did."   *Adoptee*

"I had no idea there were so many other birth mothers! Our experiences were similar in so many ways. I cried and cried all the way home from the meeting."   *Birth parent*

"We worried a lot about how the adoption would go. Knowing people who had gone through the process and could give us hints and support was really helpful."   *Adoptive parent*

Validation of one's feelings is crucial in adoption. Many triad members feel isolated and don't talk about their adoption feelings or experiences. Hearing how other people feel and having your own feelings validated is comforting to triad members.

Support and Connection

"The adoptees I met locally and on the Internet were my saving grace during the search and now in reunion. Interacting with adoptees gave me the self-esteem and courage I needed to attempt contact with my son. They loved me so much and said things like 'I hope my birth mom is just like you!' That gave me hope that my son might see in me what they saw and that possibly, he could learn to love me too."   *Birth parent*

Support and connection with others is very important for adoption triad members. To be with people who understand your feelings can be very comforting. Support can come in many forms, including support groups, adoption conferences, books, therapy, writing, and relationships.

"If not for Joe, I never would have survived the relinquishment. We started dating seven months after my daughter was born. Although he knew about my 'secret,' he never mentioned it until I was ready to talk about it. He has been the best thing that could have happened to my life! He has been my shoulder to cry on whenever the pain was too much to deal with on my own. We married three years after the birth of my daughter."

Birth parent

Some triad members find relationships with someone who is not involved in adoption but who can understand the vast range of emotions that go along with adoption issues. These relationships allow the triad member to heal in a safe and secure environment.

Types of Healing

"Late at night, I lie in bed nestled among my pillows. I do another visualization. I close my eyes and breathe deeply. I weave a bridge of light from my heart to my daughter's heart. Many strands of pink and white light connect us. I imagine I am pregnant again and gently speak to her inside of me, 'I love you. I understand now why you're angry at me. I'm so sorry I couldn't keep you. Let's try and do it differently.' This helps me to feel like I am working on our relationship in a loving and healing way." Birth parent

It is important that triad members choose a method of healing that they will respond to and find useful. Some people may want to use imagery or writing or role-playing. Others may find therapy, reading, or going to adoption conferences helpful. Different methods of healing may be effective at different times.

Respect for Other Triad Members

"Am I upset with how the adoptive parents handled my son when trouble arose? You bet I am! Most of the measures inflicted on my son to curb his rebelliousness I would not have chosen or seen as necessary. But I also believe that the adoptive parents did what they thought was best. They are good people, and their love for him is obvious." Birth parent who found son in prison

It is easy to judge from a distance. It is impossible to know another person's life as intimately as one's own. We all have ideas about how we would handle certain situations. However, we don't really know what we would actually do in a situation until we find ourselves in it.

"I was threatened by my daughter's birth mother and worried about who my daughter would go to in times of need. It took some time, but after a while and numerous conversations, I began to realize the depth of pain that Sandy, the birth mother, was feeling."
                                                          Adoptive parent

Adoption triad members owe it to themselves and to the other members of their personal triad to respect each other's point of view. Triad members come to adoption with some similar feelings and issues that can be shared and used to create a common ground for healing.

Growth
"For me, having been adopted and raised in a family with a natural child has been a difficult, yet growing experience."
                                                          Adoptee

Growth and strength can come from having to deal with difficult issues in one's life. All triad members have gone through a lot. Using and learning from the adoption experience is healing.

"I will always be an adoptee. I can't change that. The best I can do is try to heal my wounds and deal with relationships the best I can."
                                                          Adoptee

There are many issues in adoption that cannot be fully resolved. The dualities of adoption force triad members to realistically work toward the goal of accepting and integrating adoption issues and feelings.

"Now we must forgive all who have had a hand in this and start creating our own memories."
                                        Letter to adoptee from birth mother

Growth in adoption also involves forgiving oneself and the other triad members. Everyone involved in adoption did the best they could with the information they had at the time.

Seeking Help

"I always thought that alcoholism was my problem. But then, after seven years of recovery, I realize that adoption is also a huge issue, maybe the issue."   Adoptee

"I decided to go into therapy when I started having problems with my son. Our reunion wasn't going as well as I had hoped. I took everything he said so personally. My therapist helped me to communicate more directly with him, and it's made a big difference."   Birth parent

"We just didn't know what to do. We had heard about attachment disorders in adopted kids and wondered if it would help our child. It was a relief to meet a therapist who knew what to do."   Adoptive parent

Every adoption triad member will have issues and feelings about adoption. These feelings and issues present themselves differently from person to person, but one way of dealing with them is to seek out psychotherapy. Psychotherapists are trained to help people explore their feelings, communicate more effectively, and expand relationship skills.

Choosing a Therapist

"I went to three different therapists when I decided to start therapy. I asked them about adoption issues, and two of them kept saying that my adoptive family was the family to focus on. They just didn't get that being adopted was an issue for me."
                    Adoptee

Clients need to feel comfortable in a therapeutic situation. It is appropriate to interview potential psychotherapists by asking questions, considering the therapist's responses, and by sensing one's own comfort level with the therapist. The way a therapist responds can be just as important as the content of what they say.

"I wanted to find a therapist that understood how important searching for my birth mother was to me."   Adoptee

Triad members will have special needs in therapy. Because most therapists have not had formal training in adoption issues, clients need to ask questions about a therapist's education and experience in adoption.

"I spent most of my time in therapy educating my therapist about adoption issues. She kept saying that it was all so interesting and that she felt bad for me."   Birth parent

Therapy is for the client, not the therapist. It is not a triad member's duty to educate a therapist about adoption issues. Therapists are responsible for gathering the necessary information and education they need to help their clients. Ultimately, the client must decide if they are getting what they need out of therapy.

"We found our therapist through the adoptive parents support group we go to. It was important to us that we work with someone who knew about adoptive families. She had had a lot of experience with adoption and was able to help us through some difficult times."   Adoptive parent

There are various ways to get referrals to therapists who know about adoption issues. Some adoption organizations have resource and referral lists for therapists in different areas. Ask other triad members for referrals or go to lectures and seminars where therapists are speaking on adoption issues.

Therapy for Your Adopted Child

"We finally went to a child psychologist because we didn't know what else to do. James was getting in trouble in school and was not able to follow rules. The psychologist helped us to understand what James was feeling and why he might be acting out. It helped, because by that time we were at the end of our ropes."   *Adoptive parent*

Children let us know how they're feeling by acting out behaviorally. Because they don't have the verbal skills to say what is wrong, they sometimes show parents and those around them that all is not right. Therapy can help a family interpret and understand what the child is trying to convey and can shed light on family dynamics. A child's emotions and behaviors can be addressed in therapy while parents can learn how to interact with the child more effectively.

"It took us a while to find a therapist who worked with children who also knew anything about adoption."   *Adoptive parent*

When interviewing therapists for an adopted child, make sure that the therapist specializes in child therapy and knows about adoption issues. These factors will be crucial to the outcome of the therapy. A therapist who is seeing a child will also want to talk with the parents and include them in part of the therapy. This is for the benefit of the child and helps the family to function more smoothly together.

13: The Future of Adoption

"We need birth mothers to get over their guilt feelings and adoptive parents to stop feeling threatened. We've got a long way to go."
Adoptee

Understanding Adoption Issues

"If we knew then what we know now, life would have been easier for all of us. Now we can see where our lack of information about adoption gave us blind spots."
Adoptive parent

It is crucial that people in the adoption triad understand the issues involved in adoption. Feelings and emotions will surface one way or another for all triad members. Each triad member has a responsibility to learn about adoption and to teach others about it. Remember that there is no avoiding situations or feelings when one is living the adoption experience.

Changes in Adoption Practice

"I can totally understand my birth mother needing to give me up - it was the 1950s and she was unmarried and young. I still don't like it, but I can understand it. She didn't really have many choices then."
Adoptee

Adoption originally began as a solution for orphans and for children who could not be raised by their birth parents. Adoption was for the benefit of the child. Adoption has changed drastically over time. Society has changed its moral views, birth control has changed, and the options for pregnant women have expanded.

"When I hear about birth mothers today being able to choose from many adoptive parents, I feel as if I was cheated. I was treated as if I was the scum of the earth and didn't deserve to

raise my child. Now birth mothers get to have a relationship with their kids. They're lucky."   *Birth parent*

The tables have turned in adoption. In the past, there were more babies available for adoption than people who wanted to adopt. Now, there are more people who want to adopt than women who want to relinquish their babies for adoption. Pregnant women who are considering adoption can now choose who will raise their child and can make requests concerning contact and visitation.

"Even though we were desperate to adopt, we decided against going with one birth mother who was married and already had three kids. We just couldn't see taking this child away from his brothers and sister."   *Adoptive parent*

In the past, birth parents and adoptive parents did not communicate with each other before, during, or after the adoption. Professionals acted as intermediaries between the families and handled the details of the adoption. Today more communication is possible between the two families. It is important to take advantage of this, because it will help all parties feel more comfortable with each other and the choices they are making.

Adoption as a Business
"I couldn't believe people were actually advertising for babies in a national newspaper! The ads were soliciting pregnant women and offering wonderful homes for their babies via 1-800 numbers. What has the world come to?"   *Adoptee*

Adoption today has become a business for enterprising entrepreneurs. What was once the domain of those trained in the emotional aspects of human relationships has been transformed to a commercial arena in which the highest bidder wins. People now advertise and network to obtain babies. We have created an environment in which money determines who will be parents.

The Adoption Reform Movement

"Adoption really needs to catch up with the times. Triad members don't want to be lied to anymore."

Adoption professional

Many people believe that adoption continues to be in need of reform. The adoption reform movement is composed of triad members and adoption professionals who want to see honesty and openness in adoption.

"We had to change with the times. People were wanting open adoptions, and our agency decided to change our policies. We would be out of business if we only did closed adoptions."

Adoption professional

Adoptions of the past were closed and shrouded in secrecy. Today many adoption attorneys and agencies are facilitating open adoptions where information is expected and exchanged between the birth family and the adoptive family.

Open Records

"We adoptees did not sign that legal document put together by lawyers, doctors, and both sets of parents. Yet we can't get to our own original birth certificates because they are sealed to us. Reminds me and others of being sold into slavery, which was abolished in 1865."   *Adoptee*

Adoptees are the only American citizens who do not have access to their original birth certificates. Adoptees are issued amended birth certificates that name their adoptive parents as their biological parents. The adoptee's original birth certificate is considered a closed record and is sealed by court order.

"We need a way to have updated medical information put into our files to be sure that we get it. We need to know about medical conditions in our birth families - things like heart conditions, diabetes, glaucoma, and many other ills that do not show up until later years in people."   Adoptee

Closed records prevent adoptees from gaining important medical information that may be crucial to their health. A birth parent who was healthy at age seventeen may not remain so later in life. As more and more diseases and medical conditions are found to be passed on genetically, having medical information about oneself allows adoptees to make choices and decisions that could be life-enhancing and even lifesaving.

"I have been in good health my whole life. That's why I didn't give my medical history much thought. It wasn't until I became pregnant that I realized how important genetic information is. My child could be at medical risk because I don't know anything about my birth family's history. That doesn't seem fair."
Adoptee

"I'm still not sure why records were sealed in the first place. I didn't want to be removed from my child's life like I never existed."   Birth parent

Not having one's medical history is risky. Future generations are also at risk when medical information is unknown. The unknown is always more frightening than the known. Adoptees without current medical information are left wondering about their health and the health of their children. Closed records present false information on paper while the truth lives on in the hearts of each adoptee, birth parent, and adoptive parent.

Surrogacy

"I never felt as if the baby was mine. I was having this child for them. I went into it knowing what my part was."

Surrogate mother

A surrogate mother is a woman who becomes pregnant and carries a baby for a couple. The surrogate mother agrees to turn the baby over after birth to the couple who have contracted with her and paid her a fee for her services. Surrogacy raises many ethical and emotional issues. Some would say that a woman who agrees to be a surrogate mother is essentially a "womb for hire" and is being exploited. Others would say that she is giving a couple a gift that only she can give.

"We pursued surrogacy because my husband really wanted our child to have his genes. Since I was the one having the infertility problem, it seemed like the way to go."

Mother via surrogacy

People considering surrogacy must be aware of all the possibilities during the surrogacy process and after the child is born. What if the surrogate mother changes her mind and wants to keep the baby? What effect will having a surrogate mother have on the child? Who will know about the surrogacy? What will the child be told about the surrogacy?

"We have mixed feelings about telling our child. I wish we didn't have to tell him anything."   *Parent via surrogacy*

The emotional issues of surrogacy resemble those of adoption. A couple contemplating surrogacy needs to be prepared to tell the child the truth of his or her beginnings. What we know about adoption applies to surrogacy in terms of the benefits of honesty and the damage of secrecy.

Donor Insemination/Egg Donation

"At my age the choices were very slim. I had no viable eggs and my husband was younger than I was. We decided on egg donation because I wanted to have the experience of being pregnant."   Mother via egg donation

Donor insemination is the use of a known or unknown person's sperm for the purposes of conception. Egg donation involves the use of eggs from a known or unknown egg donor for the purposes of conception. Some couples who want to conceive a child with at least one parent's genetic material may choose donor insemination or egg donation. For some couples or for single women, this is the only possible way to have children who are biologically related to the parent.

"We chose to go with donor insemination with a man we knew because, being a lesbian couple, we thought it would be an easier route than adoption. We also wanted our child to know his biological history and we knew that the donor wanted to be a part of our child's life."   Parent via insemination

Some of the issues that need to be addressed when considering donor insemination or egg donation are: Will the donor be known or anonymous? If anonymous, is there the opportunity in the future to contact the donor if medical or emotional questions arise? If known, will the donor have contact with the child, and how will those arrangements be understood? What will the child be told about his or her beginnings?

"Sometimes I think about people who were born by donor insemination and I feel sorry for them. It is hard enough being an adoptee trying to find my birth family, but to never be able to

know your genetic history would be horrible. At least I have a chance of finding people who are biologically related to me."
                                                                    Adoptee

Those involved in donor insemination and egg donation can learn from those involved in adoption. Honesty enhances relationships and interactions in families. Secrecy damages intimacy and forces people to live in fear of the truth coming out.

Impact of Infertility Treatments

"If someone wants a child, we will do everything we can to help them make that dream come true."   *Infertility doctor*

Infertility treatments are a medical answer to the emotional desire to want to have children. The extent to which people will go in infertility treatment shows how strong this desire for biological children can be. Those who pursue medical treatment for infertility can spend countless hours and enormous amounts of money trying to reach their dream. The emotional impact can be extreme.

"He is our miracle child. We went through a lot, but to see his smiling face makes it all worthwhile."   *Parent*

Is reaching the dream worth it? If you speak to parents of children conceived through infertility treatment, undoubtedly you will receive a positive reply. To want something for so long and so intensely and to finally receive it feels like a miracle.

"I really worry about those babies who were conceived through infertility treatments. What would it be like to know that you began with four other siblings but only you survived?" Adoptee

What is the impact of infertility treatments on the baby, the child, the adult? What would that baby want to tell us about how it feels to have been produced by medical intervention? What will that adult be able to tell us about the long term effects of infertility treatment? We don't know the answers to these questions yet, but in the future we will.

Ethical and Moral Responsibilities

"When I hear about all the infertility procedures that people will go through, it astounds me. I get very concerned about the child and what a child will think and feel about all of it. What is it like for a child to learn that he started life outside his mother's body and that his genetic material comes from people he doesn't even know?"   Childbirth educator

What are our ethical and moral responsibilities in the area of assisted reproduction and adoption? How old is too old to parent a child? Whose egg, sperm, and body are being used to produce a child? What will the effect of all these hi-tech procedures be on the child or on the person in adult life?

"In the beginning, you think that the first procedure will work. Then you hope that the next one will. Then you pray that you will have enough stamina and money to do the next procedure. It's amazing how far you will go."   Infertility patient

Children are not experimental laboratory rats. Infertility doctors are not gods or the givers of life. Questions to ask oneself when going through hi-tech medical procedures are "Who am I doing this for?" and "How comfortable am I with this procedure?" Sometimes it is hard to know when to stop going to the next procedure because one has gone so far already.

"When will all this stop? And who is really to blame? Is it the doctors or is it the patients who are driving these procedures? And who is ultimately responsible for the outcomes?"

Response to newspaper article

More and more ethical and moral issues have presented themselves with the kind of hi-tech treatments that are available today. Along with this "progress" come the grimmer aspects. Infertility doctors are accused of taking patient's eggs, embryos, or sperm and giving them to other unknowing patients, all under the guise of bestowing the "miracle of life." As medical science expands its horizons, the moral and ethical responsibilities also expand and need to be addressed.

14: An Ideal Adoption

"Whatever happened to the best interests of the child?" Adoptee

Ideal Adoption

"I have this fantasy about going through my adoption again and being able to make it different. I would want my birth parents and my adoptive parents to meet. I would want them to talk about what is best for me and for them to agree that I needed them all in my life. I would want them to all get along and come together because they love me. Yeah, I know, pretty outlandish fantasy, huh?" Adoptee

The ideal adoption situation has a number of components. These parts, if they all work together, can make the adoption experience better for all involved. The following is an explanation of the ideal adoption components.

Adults Acting Like Adults

"Adoption scares me. You hear all those stories about birth mothers taking advantage of adoptive parents and about adoptive parents taking advantage of birth parents. It's hard to trust that adoption can work." Pre-adoptive parent

In an ideal adoption, the adults act like adults. This means that above all else, the adults keep the best interests of the child at heart. This principle determines their thoughts, actions, and behaviors. Acting like an adult involves maturity, the desire to negotiate for everyone's best interest, insight into one's own personality, and the ability to understand what another person may be experiencing.

Child as Witness

"I wonder what my parents were thinking when they knew they were going to adopt me. I wonder what my birth mother was feeling."   *Adoptee*

One way to help the adults act like adults is to imagine that the child is witnessing all that is happening in the adoption. This includes the adults' conversations, thoughts, and feelings. It is especially important to imagine the child witnessing the thoughts and feelings that the adoptive parents and the birth parents have about each other.

No Money Exchanged

"My child came home the other day and asked me how much he cost. I didn't know what he was talking about. When I asked him what he meant, he said that the kids at school said that adopted kids were bought. They said that parents go to attorneys and give them money and come home with a baby."

Adoptive parent

In an ideal adoption, no money is exchanged. This eliminates finances being a factor in parenting. If there is no exchange of money, then there is no real or imagined buying and selling of children.

Honesty

"I have spent my whole life chasing the fantasy of who my birth parents were. Now that I know them, I can relax and spend that energy more productively."   *Adoptee*

In an ideal adoption, there are no secrets. No secrets mean no need for amended birth certificates, no fantasy stories about birth parents, and no lying to children about their beginnings. Honesty is easier than secrecy and takes much less energy. The truth does set you free.

Keeping Kinship Ties

"Our kids are so used to having their birth family around that the birth family is treated the same way we are - the kids are too busy with their friends to spend time at home with any of us!"
Adoptive parent

In an ideal adoption, the kinship ties are respected and people are added to the family, not removed. Keeping kinship ties means that adoptees have access to the members of their birth family and adoptive family. There is no need for closed adoptions or secrecy about who's who. Everyone is part of the family.

Truly for the Child

"Are we trying to find homes for needy kids or kids for needy parents?"
Adoption professional

The adoptee is the one triad member who has not been consulted about the choice of adoption. It is important that the parties who are choosing adoption, the birth parents and the adoptive parents, consider the needs of the child and attempt to provide the best environment possible for the adoptee. In essence, an ideal adoption is an adoption that is truly for the child.

Suggested Reading

General

Arms, Suzanne. *Adoption: A Handful of Hope*. Berkeley, CA: Celestial Arts, 1990.

Blau, Eric. *Stories of Adoption*. Portland, OR: New Sage Press, 1993.

Burgess, Linda Cannon. *The Art of Adoption*. New York: W. W. Norton, 1981.

Franklin, Lynn C. *May the Circle be Unbroken: An Intimate Journey into the Heart of Adoption*. New York: Harmony Books, 1998.

Lifton, Betty Jean. *Lost & Found: The Adoption Experience*. New York: HarperCollins, 1988.

Pavao, Joyce Maguire. *The Family of Adoption*. Boston: Beacon Press, 1998.

Severson, Randolph W. *Adoption: Philosophy and Experience*. Dallas, TX: House of Tomorrow Productions, 1994.

Sorosky, Arthur D., Baran, Annette, and Pannor, Reuben. *The Adoption Triangle*. San Antonio, TX: Corona Publishing, 1984.

Wadia-Ells, Susan, ed. *The Adoption Reader: Birth Mothers, Adoptive Mothers and Adopted Daughters Tell Their Stories*. Seattle: Seal Press, 1995.

Adoptees

Andersen, Robert. *Second Choice: Growing Up Adopted*. Chesterfield, MO: Badger Hill Press, 1993.

Gravelle, Karen, and Fischer, Susan. *Where Are My Birth Parents?: A Guide for Teenage Adoptees*. New York:Walker and Company, 1993.

Lifton, Betty Jean. *Journey Of The Adopted Self: A Quest For Wholeness*. New York: Basis Books, 1994.

Soll, Joe. *Adoption Healing*. Baltimore: Gateway Press, 2000.

Verrier, Nancy Newton. *The Primal Wound: Understanding the Adopted Child*. Baltimore: Gateway Press, 1993.

Birth Parents

Barton, Elisa M. *Confessions of a Lost Mother*. Baltimore: Gateway Press, 1996.

Carlini, Heather. *Birth Mother Trauma: A Counseling Guide for Birthmothers*. British Columbia, Canada: Morning Side Publishing, 1992.

Franklin, Lynn C. with Ferber, Elizabeth. *May the Circle be Unbroken.* New York: Harmony Books, 1998.

Hughes, Ann H. Soul Connection: *A Birth Mother's Healing Journey.* Baltimore: Gateway Press, 1999.

Jones, Merry Bloch. *Birthmothers: Women Who Have Relinquished Babies for Adoption Tell Their Stories.* Chicago: Chicago Review Press, 1993.

Mason, Mary Martin. *Out of the Shadows: Birthfathers' Stories.* Edina, MN: O.J. Howard Publishing, 1995.

Moorman, Margaret. *Waiting to Forget.* New York: W.W. Norton, 1996.

Roles, Patricia. *Saying Goodbye to a Baby, Volume 1: The Birthparent's Guide to Loss and Grief in Adoption.* Washington, DC: Child Welfare League of America, 1989.

Schaefer, Carol. *The Other Mother: A Woman's Love for the Child She Gave Up for Adoption.* New York: Soho Press, 1991.

Taylor, Patricia. *Shadow Train: A Journey Between Relinquishment and Reunion.* Baltimore, MD: Gateway Press, 1995.

Waldron, Jan L. *Giving Away Simone: A Memoir.* New York: Times Books, 1995.

Adoptive Parenting

Fahlberg, Vera I. *A Child's Journey Through Placement.* Indianapolis, IN: Perspectives Press, 1991.

Jewett, Claudia L. *Adopting the Older Child.* Boston: Harvard Common Press, 1978.

Jewett, Claudia L. *Helping Children Cope with Separation and Loss.* Harvard, MA: Harvard Common Press, 1982.

Melina, Lois Ruskai. *Making Sense of Adoption: A Parent's Guide..* New York: Harper & Row, 1989.

Melina, Lois Ruskai. *Raising Adopted Children: A Manual for Adoptive Parents.* New York: Harper & Row, 1986.

Siegel, Stephanie E. *Parenting Your Adopted Child: A Complete and Loving Guide.* Encino, CA: SES Publishing, 1997.

van Gulden, Holly, and Rabb, Lisa M. Bartels. *Real Parents, Real Children: Parenting the Adopted Child.* New York: Crossroad, 1995.

Wolff, Jana. *Secret Thoughts of an Adoptive Mother.* Honolulu: Vista Communications, 2000.

Loss and Grief

Kubler-Ross, Elisabeth. *On Death and Dying.* New York: Macmillan, 1969.

Rando, Therese A., ed. *Parental Loss of a Child.* Champaign, IL: Research Press, 1986.

Roles, Patricia. *Saying Goodbye to a Baby, Volume 2: A Counselor's Guide to Birthparent Loss and Grief in Adoption.* Washington, DC: Child Welfare League of America, 1989.

Silverman, Phyllis R. *Helping Women Cope with Grief.* Beverly Hills: Sage Publications, 1981.

Search and Reunion

Demuth, Carol L. *Courageous Blessing: Adoptive Parents and the Search.* Garland, TX: Aries Center, 1993.

Gediman, Judith S. and Brown, Linda P. *BirthBond: Reunions Between Birthparents and Adoptees.* Far Hills, NJ: New Horizon Press, 1989.

Gunderson, Ted L. with McGovern, Roger. *How to Locate Anyone Anywhere: Without Leaving Home.* New York: Dutton, 1989.

McColm, Michelle. *Adoption Reunions: A Book for Adoptees, Birth Parents and Adoptive Families.* Toronto: Second Story Press, 1993.

Rillera, Mary Jo. *The Adoption Searchbook: Techniques for Tracing People.* Westminster, CA: Triadoption Publications, 1981.

Rillera, Mary Jo. *The Reunion Book.* Westminster, CA: Triadoption Publications, 1991.

Saffian, Sarah. *Ithaka: A Daughter's Memoir of Being Found.* New York: Basic Books, 1998.

Sanders, Patricia, and Sitterly, Nancy. *Search Aftermath and Adjustments.* Santa Ana, CA, 1981.

Stiffler, LaVonne Harper. *Synchronicity & Reunion: The Genetic Connection of Adoptees and Birthparents.* Hobe Sound, FL: FEA Publishing, 1992.

Strauss, Jean A.S. *Birthright: The Guide To Search and Reunion for Adoptees, Birthparents, and Adoptive Parents.* New York: Penguin Books, 1994.

Open Adoption

Gritter, James L., ed. *Adoption Without Fear*. San Antonio, TX: Corona Publishing, 1989.

Melina, Lois Ruskai and Roszia, Sharon Kaplan. *The Open Adoption Experience*. New York: HarperCollins, 1993.

Silber, Kathleen and Dorner, Patricia Martinez. *Children of Open Adoption*. San Antonio, TX: Corona Publishing, 1989.

Silber, Kathleen and Speedlin, Phylis. *Dear Birthmother, Thank You for our Baby*. San Antonio, TX: Corona Publishing, 1982.

International Adoption

Bishoff, Tonya and Rankin, Jo, eds. *Seeds From a Silent Tree: An Anthology by Korean Adoptees*. Glendale, CA: Pandal Press, 1997.

Dodds, Peter. *Outer Search Inner Journey: An Orphan and Adoptee's Quest*. Puyallup, WA: Aphrodite Publishing, 1997.

Developmental

Brodzinsky, David M., Schechter, Marshall D. and Henig, Robin Marantz. *Being Adopted: The Lifelong Search for Self*. New York: Doubleday, 1992.

Rosenberg, Elinor B. *The Adoption Life Cycle: The Children and Their Families Through the Years*. New York: The Free Press, 1992.

Clinical / Research

Brodzinsky, David M., and Schechter, Marshall D., eds. *The Psychology of Adoption*. New York: Oxford University Press, 1990.

Gross, Harriet E. and Sussman, Marvin B., eds. *Families And Adoption*. New York: Haworth Press, 1997.

Kirk, H. David. *Adoptive Kinship: A Modern Institution in Need of Reform*. Port Angeles, WA: Ben-Simon Publications, 1981.

Kirk, H. David. *Shared Fate: A Theory & Method of Adoptive Relationships*. Port Angeles, WA: Ben-Simon Publications, 1984.

Reitz, Miriam, and Watson, Kenneth. *Adoption and the Family System*. New York: Guilford Press, 1992.

Winkler, Robin C., Brown, Dirck W., van Keppel, Margaret, and Blanchard, Amy. *Clinical Practice in Adoption*. Elmsford, NY: Pergamon Press, 1988.

Pre- and Perinatal Psychology

Chamberlain, David B. *Babies Remember Birth.* Los Angeles: Jeremy P. Tarcher, 1988.

Huxley, Archera Laura, and Ferrucci, Piero. *The Child of Your Dreams.*Rochester, VT: Destiny Books, 1992.

Janus, Ludwig. *The Enduring Effects of Prenatal Experience: Echoes from the Womb.* Northvale, NJ: Jason Aronson, 1997.

Leboyer, Frederick. *Birth Without Violence.* New York: Alfred A. Knopf, 1976.

Nilsson, Lennart. *A Child is Born.* New York: DTP/Seymour Lawrence, 1990.

Verny, Thomas, and Weintraub, Pamela. *Nurturing the Unborn Child: A Nine-Month Program for Soothing, Stimulating, and Communicating with Your Baby.* New York: Delta, 1991.

Verny, Thomas R. with Kelly, John. *The Secret Life of the Unborn Child.* New York: Dell, 1981.

Art / Poetry / Rituals

Flax, Carol. *Some (M)other Stories: A Parent(hetic)al Tale.* Daytona Beach, FL: Southeast Museum of Photography, 1995.

Mason, Mary Martin. *Designing Rituals of Adoption for the Religious and Secular Community.* Minneapolis: Resources for Adoptive Parents, 1995.

Partridge, Penny Callan. *An Adoptee's Dreams: Poems and Stories.* Baltimore, MD: Gateway Press, 1995.

Severson , Randolph W. *Adoption: Charms and Rituals for Healing.* Dallas, TX: House of Tomorrow Productions, 1991.

Schulz, David. *non-identifying social, genetic report.* Brooklyn, NY: Hammer Productions, 1999.

Donor Insemination

Baran, Annette and Pannor, Reuben. *Lethal Secrets: The Psychology of Donor Insemination.* New York: Armisted Press, 1993.

Noble, Elizabeth. *Having Your Baby by Donor Insemination: A Complete Resource Guide.* Boston: Houghton Mifflin, 1987.

Surrogacy

Atwood, Margaret. *The Handmaid's Tale.* Boston, MA: Houghton Mifflin, 1986.

Chesler, Phyllis. *Sacred Bond: The Legacy of Baby M.* New York: Times Books, 1988.

Fiction

Homes, A.M. *In a Country of Mothers.* New York: Alfred A. Knopf,
1993.
Kagan, Elaine. *Somebody's Baby.* NewYork: William Morrow, 1998.
Kingsolver, Barbara. *Pigs in Heaven.* New York: HarperCollins, 1993.
Lipman, Elinor. *Then She Found Me.* New York: Pocket Books, 1990.

Adoption Reform

Griffith, Keith C. *The Right To Know Who You Are: Reform of
Adoption Law with Honesty Openness and Integrity.* Ontario,
Canada: Katherine Kimbell, 1991.
Riben, Marsha. S*hedding Light on the Dark Side of Adoption.* Detroit:
Harlo Press, 1988.
Solinger, Rickie. *Wake Up Little Susie: Single Pregnancy and Race
Before Roe v. Wade.* New York: Routledge, 1992.

About the Author

Marlou Russell, Ph.D. is a psychologist and Marriage and Family therapist in private practice in Santa Monica, California. She provides psychotherapy and counseling for adoptees, birth parents, and adoptive families. She facilitates support/therapy groups for adult adoptees and birth parents and offers consultation to professionals in the field of psychology on adoption issues.

Dr. Russell is a speaker at adoption and psychological conferences around the country. Her articles on adoption have appeared in various publications.

Dr. Russell is a member of the Adoptee's Liberty Movement Association, American Adoption Congress, Concerned United Birthparents, Council for Equal Rights in Adoption, Kinship Alliance, and Resolve.

She is a member of the following professional associations: California Psychological Association, Los Angeles County Psychological Association, American Association of Marriage and Family Therapists, California Association of Marriage and Family Therapists, and the Los Angeles Chapter of the California Association of Marriage and Family Therapists.

Dr. Russell is listed in *Who's Who of American Women, Who's Who of Emerging Leaders in America, Who's Who in Medicine and Health Care,* and *Who's Who in the World.*

Contacting the Author

Dr. Russell offers counseling, consultation, speaking and writing on adoption issues.

Marlou Russell, Ph.D.

www.marlourussellphd.com

Facebook: Marlou Russell PhD

11831533R0012

Made in the USA
Lexington, KY
05 November 2011